The Journey of a Thousand Miles

Begins With a Trip to the Post Office

MJ Blehart

The Journey of a Thousand Miles
Begins With a Trip to the Post Office
Copyright © 2017 MJ Blehart.

ISBN-13: 978-0692909638

ISBN-10: 069290963X

Published 2017 by MJ Blehart and Argent Hedgehog Press

Argent
Hedgehog
Press

Published in the United States of America

www.mjblehart.com

I want to thank Jody for suggesting I write this out in the first place, Cathy for her encouragement when joining in the discussion in the parking lot about it, Kristin for her constant support, Niki for her initial approval of my telling of certain parts of the story, and everyone who read the updates about my progress on LiveJournal (remember when that was a relevant place?), and the incredible encouragement you all gave me. I would like to thank the folks at National Novel Writer's Month (NaNoWRiMo.org) for providing the impetus for writing it out.

I want to thank my mom, my dad, my sister, my stepfather and stepmother for all of your amazing support through this difficult experience all those years ago.

I'd also like to thank my editor, Ned.

Last, but certainly not least, I need to thank Chuck. You are missed, my friend.

Table of Contents

Prologue – To protect the innocent and reveal the -- inane, maybe?

This is a true story, of one man, picked by the powers-that-be, to live a life unlike any other.

But isn't that the case with, well, everyone?

My life is not the same as your life - or anyone else's. Life is a unique, individual experience that we can share with others in many times and many ways and many formats, but no matter all that, we always live our own life, and no one else's. Some lives are probably better than others. I have come to believe that you get pretty much what you give, and it's the everyday, mundane choices that give and take our power, make us happy or sad, energetic or depressed. We are on an endless quest to understand our lives, and how they affect not only ourselves, but those we surround ourselves with.

I have made some good, some bad, some stupid, some brilliant, and some pretty unexceptional choices in my life. I have even, from time to time, chosen not to make a choice, either. All those choices and non-choices have shaped who I am, and both guided and misguided me to some very interesting places - and interesting, to quote Joss Whedon's *Serenity*, can mean, "Oh god, oh god, we're all gonna die."

This is a true story. For real. Yes, names have been changed to protect people who may not want their roles in this story from my life explored or detailed, and who needs the lawsuits? Of course, I have only my own memory of the events to go on, and while I am sure that some might argue my take on the situation is not theirs, and may not even be the truth, as they remember it, they are what I recall, and it *is*, after all, my life, and my story.

Herein is a whole bunch of crazy stuff that I don't think I could possibly make up. Get comfortable, maybe have a beverage and a light snack handy, and step into a life that, while unique, may not have started out so differently from your own.

Chapter 1 – You just never know what to expect.

So this is what I get for not being lazy.

I mean, c'mon, who knew a quarter mile walk to the post office could end up in months of pain, suffering, and physical therapy? Not me, obviously.

Step back into the time machine with me. Let's borrow Mr. Peabody's "Wayback" machine, shall we? His boy Sherman can just stay home, thanks.

It's November, 1999. I am between jobs, and just at the start of yet another of my yo-yo weight loss maneuvers. I have written all the checks to pay my bills, but they need to be mailed out. The post office is a whopping quarter mile from my home and, though I certainly don't recall it, the weather is apparently decent.

I need to lose weight, a million pounds or so. Well ok, maybe more like forty, but that's neither here nor there. So rather than drive, I'll just walk to the post office.

How in the fuck did I get here?

"Where's here?" you ask.

"Here" is a hospital bed, they tell me, in Manhattan - and it's been a week or so since the accident.

Accident? I remember no accident.

But then, I don't seem to remember a *lot* of things.

My friends relay a number of stories about things I said over the past week.

When the doctors said, "Warren, open your eyes," apparently my answer was, "Just put it on my Visa!"

Do I recall that? No.

"I think I'm just going to fold it up into teeny tiny little pieces," Jill claims I said. Really? So what the fuck was I talking about at that point?

"Warren, c'mon buddy, gimme a sign," Bob claimed he chided me. He tells me I rolled over some, moaned and griped about the catheter.

Now, somewhere in all of that, I seem to remember waking in the middle of the night and thinking it was all just a bad drama. I *am* an actor, after all – or at least played one, from time to time, in High School and College. Anyhow, it's a bad drama, so I remove the IV from my arm, and some protective wrapping from the other, and reach for my in-traction leg. That is not doable. I collapse and pass back out.

Sometime soon after that, my doctors reduced my morphine drip.

I don't recall when, exactly, I woke up. I don't know when I came around for real and started to be aware of my surroundings, but it happened, and I realized my mom was there.

Why is my mom in New York, anyhow? Shouldn't she still be in Chicago, at work?

Next question*: How come I am very uncomfortable, feel like I've been in bed for a week, and can't remember why I am here*?

Next question: *Why is my right leg in traction*?

Next question: *How come my right arm isn't working? Why won't it move*?

Last question: *What the fuck happened?*

We've never put together all the pieces. Hell, some pieces were missing, after all, but I am getting ahead of myself. Like I wrote earlier, I decided, on an apparently nice November day, that I was going to take a walk to the post office and mail out my bills. The quarter mile journey that walk represents is not all that treacherous, really - until you factor in the two-lane highway one must cross. Now, in all fairness, it is probable I was not, in fact, in the crosswalk. No excuse, still, for what happened.

To make a long story short (which defeats the purpose of this, in many respects), I was struck by a car, when I crossed that street.

Car versus man. Guess who wins? Yup. Not the man.

I have theorized that my right leg was clipped, and I was thus thrown. When I landed, my right shoulder connected with the curb, as did my gut. My face, of course, connected with the pavement. Ouch.

I was told that what I am experiencing is called "traumatic amnesia". Something *very* painful happened, and my mind blocked it out.

Thank you, oh grey-matter, for doing something more than just retaining useless bits of trivia, which causes people to not watch *Jeopardy!* with me.

So, after being struck by the car, I lay on the side of the road, bleeding. The guy who struck me? Well, ya know, that's not entirely fair; I presume it was a guy. But you see, I don't know. He, or, to be fair, she, didn't bother to stop. Yes, I was the victim of a hit and run. Don't know if I even made the six o'clock news. Somehow, I doubt it.

I have been told that the next car or two or three after whoever hit me also continued on their merry way. Thanks, really, people. It was the fourth car that stopped.

I believe the first responder to my accident was a priest. My mom tells me that somewhere in my morphine induced haze, the priest stopped by to check in on me.

That is only amusing when you bear in mind that I was raised Jewish. Not that my name doesn't give me away as a man of Jewish faith to most people. Though, unlike most Warrens, I am not anywhere near my sixties, yet, and I don't care all that much if those damned kids are on my lawn again.

But I digress.

Apparently, I became conscious, at some point, during said priest's visit, and made a comment to the effect of, "Oh, shit, I died and must have gone to the wrong place!"

I really hope he had a good sense of humor.

So here I am, lying in a hospital bed, and I am told that my right tibia has been shattered, my right fibula fractured, and my right clavicle is fractured as well.

I know that my clavicle is my collar bone. The tibia, and fibula, I am told, are the two bones in the leg between the knee and ankle. And, I am told, my tibia is wrecked badly.

Have I mentioned "ouch" yet?

As a result of my fractured clavicle, the nerve cluster that runs to my arm, called the brachial plexus, has been stretched.

That sounds not so bad, right? Will my one arm be longer than the other now?

No. The nerves are damaged, and that is why the arm is not working.

Okay. That is not a good thing. So the next question is, will my arm work again - and can my leg be fixed?

"Repairs are under way."

Images of a skyscraper in scaffolding come to mind. That, it turns out, will be rather apropos.

I need to go in for another surgery. It will be my second, apparently. They will be doing something or other to my leg, I guess, and then my recovery will begin in earnest.

Honestly, this part is all a little vague. I kinda remember being wheeled into the prep for the OR, and I sort of recall conversing with the doctor, or maybe it was a nurse - or it might have been an orderly. I honestly just don't remember now.

I do, however, remember that my catheter was removed. I am pretty sure the only reason that was not as painful as anticipated was because the anesthetic had kicked in. Still, that is not something I would inflict on anyone - Not even the bastard who hit me with a car. I had *far* more interesting tortures for him, or her, in mind.

Sometime following that surgery, things begin to be clearer. I start to remember friends and family visiting me, now. Apparently, at one point in all my morphine induced haze, I could not stop asking for Torrance.

Torrance was my on again, off again, on again, off again, on again, off-again-but-we're-still-sleeping-together best friend. Or girlfriend, depending on the day of the week and the phase of the moon. And apparently, at one point during all of this, my fiancé.

Well, at least that's what she told them at the hospital, so that they would let her see me during the "family only" visiting period. Tori and I have had a long, twisted, complicated love/hate relationship. Calling it imperfect would be generous. Calling it bizarre and largely fucked up would be closer to accurate, but through it all, we've still always managed to be there for one another. We'll get into that more along the way.

Following surgery number two, I have an external fixator attached to my leg. The term "external fixator" does, sort of, illicit images of medieval torture devices and, ironically, it isn't far from the reality of it. Pins have been screwed into various parts of my leg, two just below the knee, four at various points around my ankle, and two in the bottom of my foot.

That's half the fun. Various metal bars and rods are attached to said pins, a "satellite" designed to keep my bones in place while I begin to heal in a far better manner than a cast would do. The fixator has basically left me with a null area above my leg that goes about eight inches or so.

Sleeping on my stomach, which is how I normally sleep, is going to be impossible with this thing on my leg. Just inside the lovely metal scaffolding that keeps my leg in more-or-less one piece, there is a *very* unpleasant looking bit of skin. It's like there was a hole of some sort, and they have closed it over with what appears to be skin that may well have been removed from somewhere via a cheese slicer.

Oh, wait. That's more-or-less accurate. It was.

It's a skin graft, taken from my upper right thigh. It had been placed to cover what I will learn is the exit wound.

Yeah, you read that right, "exit wound." As in, the point from which my shattered tibia protruded from my body.

So I am a resident of Columbia Presbyterian Hospital for a time. And it is a fine hospital. It also happens to be a teaching hospital. That means I have a lot of doctors, and doctor-esque residents and students hovering over me during daylight hours. It was a veritable parade of lab coats.

My case presented them with a fine example of a multitude of broken bones and the expected lengthy recovery process. Not to mention the already multiple and complex surgeries they performed, to put me back together.

Insert sound effects and cheesy music from *The Six Million Dollar Man* here.

"We can rebuild him. We can make him better - stronger - faster."

That would have been nice.

Not that I am complaining. At that point I would have been happy simply with rebuilt, like I was before I learned that the human body does not fare well against a moving car.

So now I am becoming more and more aware of my surroundings, and the fact that I am in quite a lot of pain. The meds are a nice thing; they take what would be a fairly sharp and unmanageable pain and change it to a much duller, far more manageable ache. This is going to take some getting used to.

***

Once they scooped my broken body off the street, they went through my wallet, and found my dad's business card. On the plus side, we have the same last name. More than that, his card has his picture on it, and it is very, very obvious we are of the same blood line. So they called him, and he made other necessary calls. One of those calls, of course, was to my mother.

I love my mom, don't get me wrong, but she is the stereotypical Jewish mother, with the exception of the accent. We are from the Midwest, and while I have lived on the east coast a long time now, she has lived, pretty much, her whole life in the middle of the country. So just imagine the stereotype of the mom nagging, but switch out the Brooklyn accent, insert a Chicago one, and enjoy the hilarity.

Anyhow, my mom is unsurprisingly very worried, and flies out. Apparently she is staying in my apartment, which is good because that means someone is watching my cat.

So mom comes by to visit, and she's only just keeping herself together. I know it's rough, I mean her boy is barely in one piece in the hospital, and clearly did not pay attention, as a child, to the constant reminders to, "look both ways before you cross the street."

So my mom is here, Tori is here, My dad, my stepmom, my pal Bob, and even my sister has flown in.

Bob is still cracking jokes and making snarky comments around me. His girlfriend giggles at them in her usual way. Some of the other friends who have popped by have been their normal selves. No one is being too nice, everyone is acting as though aside from the scary satellite orbiting my leg, everything will be okay.

I take that as a good sign. Still being teased, still being joked with; okay, good, I am obviously not dying. Whew!

So I now learn from my doctor, a nice Jewish man with a strong German name, that I nearly lost my right foot. They could not, upon bringing me to the nearer hospital to my home, where the EMTs took me, find a pulse in my poor foot. Just when it looked like they may have no choice but to remove it, apparently my pulse was found.

That is some good news.

My fractured clavicle is less of a problem than the stretched nerve cluster. Yup, got a *really* spiffy scar across the front of my right shoulder, but the nerve damage is why my arm will not respond. That is the most fascinating and bizarre thing. You have no idea, probably, what it is like to look at your arm, lying there at your side, and while you are sending it commands to do simple things, like rise up, or bend at the elbow, or twiddle the fingers, very little is happening. A twitch here and there, but beyond that, it will not move. I push. I fight. I think really hard about it. I will it to work. I attempt to use The Force to make my arm do my mind's bidding. No good. It is very disconcerting.

"You should begin to recover the use of your arm a little bit every day," the doctor tells me. "And as it improves, in time there should be more and more function."

"Am I going to completely get back the use of my arm?" I like to ask direct questions.

He hesitates. "Possibly. Only time will tell."

Okay. Not a negative, but not the best answer I wanted.

Actually, over the next couple of days, I do begin to get back some movement in my arm. Mostly at the shoulder, and I can kind of move some of my fingers. It's better than nothing, but damn is it frustrating.

There are some minor, albeit annoying logistical problems. First and foremost, I can't get out of bed. My leg is pretty badly wrecked, so I am going to be unable to stand. I am still, as far as I know, human, and that means, from time to time, I gotta use the bathroom. I am no longer catheterized (thank god, or the gods, or the powers-that-be, but that's another topic). So I now have a bottle-thing to pee in. They actually produce a plastic bottle specifically for this purpose, I will have you know. So I am peeing into a bottle.

Oddly, don't need to poop. This might be an overshare, I realize, but when you know it is a bodily function that is supposed to occur daily, there is some concern when it is not happening for a week. Or two. Or three. But if the doctors are not showing concern about it, I'm certainly not going to worry.

So, what is going to happen now, I begin to question.

Physical therapy.

When they finish doing all they can for me here, I will be moved to a rehabilitation hospital, and begin, in earnest, my physical therapy. That should allow me to start the road to recovery, and begin work to recover use of my arm, and to get comfortable doing everyday things like standing up.

"When can I begin to walk again?"

I don't recall just how many different answers I got to that question, but I was informed that in a few months, if my healing progresses well enough, they will be performing a third surgery, this one to repair my leg. A bone graft.

"Okay, spare me the gory details. How long til I can walk again?"

If the bone graft takes, and things heal quickly enough, I will be able to start to bear weight once again, and we will take it from there. Again, they have yet to properly answer my question.

I honestly don't recall if I got the answer from a friend, or a relative, who in turn got the answer from a doctor, but somehow I have been told it will probably be one to three *years* before I am walking again.

Oh no. No no no. That's bullshit. We'll see about that.

Chapter 2 – A Little Insight into my life.

So, now seems as good a time as any to interject my social life into this tale of woe and misery. I have, since the early 1990's, been a part of a world-wide medieval recreation organization called the Society for Creative Anachronism (SCA). The SCA is, in many ways, like a big family. A big, incestuous, dysfunctional, high-school, hive-minded family, at times, but a family none-the-less. I met Torrance through the Society, as well as Jill and Bob and most of my closer friends.

In that fine organization, I take on the persona of a sixteenth century Scotsman named William MacDonald. As such, there are a number of people who call me Will far more often than Warren. Most of those people agree that I look a lot more like a Will than a Warren, whatever that means, and there is my one friend who puts it like this, "No one named Warren should be listening to Nine Inch Nails and be a fan of rollerblading." Probably true.

Anyhow, in the SCA, my favorite activity is medieval fencing. Rapier combat. Sword fighting. I love that game. Of course, being laid up in a hospital bed is not going to be very conducive to my game.

So being of a mind to get back to my life as much as possible, as soon as possible, I have to wonder, with my leg wrecked and a long recovery ahead, and a non-functional primary arm, will I be able to fence?

If my arm does not recover - I might not.

Well, no, I actually *can* fence left-handed. Not quite as well as with my right, but I can.

I blame the movie *The Princess Bride*. One of the best scenes in that movie is the sword fight between Westley (Cary Elwes) and Inigo (Many Patinkin). They deliver the best lines.

Inigo: "I know something you do not know."

Westley: "And what is that?"

Inigo: "I am not left-handed."

fight - fight - fight

Westley: "There is something I should tell you."

Inigo: "Tell me?"

Westley: "I am not left-handed either!"

Brilliant!

So I took it upon myself to learn to fence left handed. Of course, in the SCA, we sometimes fence with multiple weapons: a sword and dagger, a sword and buckler, even a sword in each hand. But when you are teaching someone new how to fence with a single sword, there is nothing quite like the satisfaction of messing with them by spending some time fighting as a lefty. Then, once you have frustrated them enough, deliver the line, "There is something you do not know. I am not left handed!"

Yup. Cheesy. Somewhat obnoxious. Borderline lame. That's me.

My extended medieval family has come by to visit from time to time, and they have treated me no differently than before. It is a good thing.

Now that I am more aware of what is going on, I have noticed that something is missing, and during one of her visits, I query my mom.

"Mom, I don't have my chain. My necklace. I know I was wearing it."

I have a chain that was a gift from my mother, grandmother, sister and stepfather that I only take off when I am in my medieval persona, and it is not on me at this moment.

"It's okay," she comforts me, then produces it, "It wasn't stolen; your father got it, and gave it to me to give back to you. I think it's okay now."

So, she puts it back on me, and I feel a bit better.

Eventually I recall that, as much as it was apparently a decent day when I left my apartment to go for this fateful jaunt, I probably had thrown on my beloved leather jacket. I query my father about that.

His eyes drop, "Sorry son…they had to cut it off you."

"They had to *what*?"

"You were a bloody mess, and they were not entirely sure where all your injuries were, so they had to cut you out of your jacket to work on you."

"Oh."

"If it makes you feel any better, I did shed a tear when I threw it out."

sigh

Now, in addition to all the visitors, the physical and occupational therapists are coming by. The physical therapist is a very attractive blonde girl. I mean, wow, she's really cute.

"Let's begin by having you raise and lower each leg."

Right. Not a problem. Left leg is up, then down. Right leg is up, and damned is that satellite thing heavy! Process repeated several times. Reps, even.

Did I mention that the therapist is really cute?

"Alright, Mr. Mushnik, let's have you stand up."

Tentatively, I swung my legs off the edge of the bed.

"Remember, all the weight has to be on the left," she reminds me sweetly.

Got it. Left leg - is - on the floor. Right leg is - heavy, but I can keep it up, if I use my left arm to hold onto the railing of the bed.

My right arm is just hanging there.

C'mon, righty, move!

"Well, this is a good start," she says.

I think that was the extent of my initial physical therapy.

The occupational therapist is the next to visit. Darker skinned, dark haired girl. Also extremely cute. You know, if all my therapists are this attractive, this is going to help speed my recovery.

So, she manipulates my arm for me, bends it, moves it, has me attempt to do some on my own. I can kind of move some fingers, slightly. My wrist twitches a bit, and I am beginning to be able to move at the shoulder.

"Pretty good," she says.

I am encouraged.

It would probably be best, though, to not let Tori know that I am attracted to these lovely therapists. But then, there are a lot of things it would be best if Tori did not know. But that's another story.

So they are nearly done with me at the hospital. That means I am soon to be moved to the rehab hospital in Rockland County. I know of that place; it's not too far from my apartment.

Mom is sticking around, and while she and my dad have been divorced for the better part of twenty two years, dad has been really good to her, and let her take my stepmom's car. Mom can't drive my car. It's a stick shift.

I remember when I was four, or so, and my mom, very pregnant with my sister, was being given a lesson in driving manual transmission by my dad. At the time, dad had a Mercedes. A two seater-convertible, even. Sweet car. I am certain it was a hand-me-down from grandpa. Grandpa loved his two-seater Mercedes.

So we're in a parking lot, and mom is behind the wheel, and dad is trying to explain clutching and shifting. At least I'm pretty sure that's what he had to be doing, since I drive manual and at the time I was too young to understand what he was attempting to teach mom. The classic Mercedes two-seater did not have a proper back seat. There was a hump back there. The top, when folded down, was partly stored in that hump. So I am sitting on the hump, not strapped in, while mom is attempting to drive stick.

Hey, this was the mid 1970's. It was a far less pussy-whipped society back then. Seat belt and car seat laws were much more lenient, if not non-existent. Anyone who has driven stick knows that the hardest thing to master is getting in and out of first gear. It is a complex process involving timing and coordination and a general sense of the engine, the clutch, and other factors.

Use the Force. Feel the engine demand to be shifted.

My mom is not a Force practitioner.

So at some point, she seriously lurches the car, and I bump my head on the hard leather seat in front of me. Crying ensues. Driving lesson ends. Mom never learned to drive stick.

Since she's staying around for a while longer, and dad has things he needs to do, he takes my car, lets my stepmom, Lucy, take his car, and has mom take Lucy's car.

They are prepping me to move to the rehab hospital. The goal will be for me to recover enough to return to my apartment, and start in-home therapy, so that I might actually return to some semblance of my life.

It dawns on me about now that I have a choice, and this leads to one of my philosophies on life in general. I am broken. And there are really only three options before me:

1. Curl up into a ball, cry a lot, and wait to die.

2. Just wait it out. Let time have its way with me. Take it as it comes.

3. Grab the bull by the horns, and fight every step of the way.

I have never opted for option 1. Even in my most depressed state, I never was suicidal. Too much left to do in this world.

Option 2 is a good option. But that is the option that means it's going to be one to three years before I can walk again, let alone fence.

Option 3 is going to be painful. But then, I'm pretty much constantly in pain at this point anyhow, so what's the difference?

If I choose option three, maybe I can get back to this thing I call my life a lot bloody faster. My doctor clears me, signs the necessary paperwork, and it is time for me to go to rehab.

Chapter 3 – Rehab isn't just for alcoholics and drug addicts.

Helen Hayes is one of the finest rehabilitation hospitals in the nation. That is a comforting fact, in especial when you consider the level of rehabilitation reassembling me is going to take.

I have what few things were with me gathered together, and my mom will be following along. So, onto the gurney and into the ambulance I go.

This would be my third trek via the back of an ambulance. The first I have no recollection of – I was somewhat of a mess at the time. The second is equally blank, since I was only a day or so from the first, and am pretty certain this is a pair of episodes I will never manage to recall.

Incidentally, there would be, years later, a fourth trek in the back of ambulance, but not due to any injury or illness of my own. We were attending a concert when a friend decided that mixing Benadryl and alcohol would make a terrific science experiment. Friend fell down and went boom, said friend's head meeting a concrete floor rather swiftly. So I got to ride in the back of the ambulance about twenty blocks through New York City.

If you are a fan of swiftly spinning amusement park rides, or any other similar vomit inducing activities, a speeding ambulance through Manhattan, when there is no traffic, is an equal thrill. Makes the unconscious treks sound all that much better, frankly. But I digress.

This, my third trip, I was awake for, and it just so happened the EMT was an attractive female.

Yes, I know that this is the third woman I have mentioned to be attractive, and each, frankly, was very different. We aren't even talking about Torrance nor Jillian at this point, but we'll cover that later. The PT was a cute blond. The OT was an attractive, exotic brunette. The EMT in the ambulance was a taller, broader dirty-blond haired woman. Very different types, and all attractive in different ways.

This is the first jaunt I have taken out of my hospital bed for more than a few seconds. Previously I have arisen and stood on my good leg for less than a minute, and I have been able to sit upright for extended periods of time. Any kind of travel was not going to be happening. But now I get to take a nice, thirty minute ambulance ride, and at least the company is pleasant.

We talk about general things. Obviously a primary topic is my accident, and my current trip to rehab. She was impressed that it had only taken me three weeks to leave the hospital. Okay, I can take that as a good sign, judging by the source. EMTs see a lot of crap that makes my accident look less horrific. Of course, conversely, they see a lot that made my situation look worse.

We turn up a large hill, and I can see the building we are approaching. It is Helen Hayes. The rehab hospital is divided into different floors for different levels of care and types of rehabilitations. Some are more complex than others. For example, as I recall it, there was a floor dedicated to the rehabilitation of brain injuries. This ranged from near paralysis to impairments from strokes and other such brain traumas.

I was to be on the first floor, mostly orthopedic and similar rehabilitation. People broken in accidents like my own, some recovering from replacements of knees and hips, and still others having lesser and greater needs. I was wheeled into the room I would be sharing with three other gentlemen. Mind you, even in the hospital I had had a private room, and at this point had been living alone for about a decade or so. A situation with three new roommates was going to prove to be interesting.

So I was moved from the gurney to the bed, and immediately there was consultation about getting me more mobile again. The plan was to put me in a powered wheelchair. Having very limited use of my right arm, and no use at all of my right leg, they deemed this the best way to get me some mobility.

My mother of course was pushing to get me moved to a more private room, but in Helen Hayes the most private would still leave me with a roommate. Thanks for trying, mom.

Within less than an hour of my arrival, it was determined that I had probably had more than enough time in a bed, and even if it meant someone would have to push me around for the time being, they opted to help me into a wheelchair. Of course it was going to take a little time to get me a powered chair. So I believe it was a nurse and an orderly who helped me into the chair.

Anyone who knows me knows that I have very little patience. I don't like to be immobilized, I like to be on the go rather constantly. It should come as no surprise that, my good foot on the ground, I started to push a bit, and see if I could maneuver the chair in the least.

Okay, good start, I can sort of use my good leg as a rudder. Mind you, my bad leg is currently elevated and pointed forward, like a lance in scaffolding. I have no doubt jousting will probably be painful. Not certain just how much pain touching the leg with any pressure will cause.

Let's take the example of a canoe in still water here. If you always paddle on the left side, you are only going to circle around. Endlessly. Same theory was expected to apply to a wheelchair. If only the left arm and left leg are available to control and steer the chair, I'm going to spend a lot of time in circles. So much for mobility.

The words of a pair of childhood heroes came to mind with regard to that situation. The first was the sage, my personal Buddha, Yoda. "Try not. Do. Or do not. There is no try." That might be my mantra, if I adopted a mantra. The other words were from a more brash source - Han Solo, "Never tell me the odds!"

Let me get this out of the way now. I am a geek. A really big geek. I have seen all the Star Wars movies, even the prequels, many, many times. And this is not my sole geekdom. Just putting that out there.

Ok, where was I?

Left arm, left leg, drag and steer with the leg, use the arm to turn the wheel. And I am not moving in circles. Soon I am across the room. It takes some effort to not just move in a circle, but I am nothing if not persistent!

Left arm, left leg, drag and steer, turn the wheel. I've returned to my starting point in less than half the time it took. I think I might have the hang of this. In minutes, I am out of the room and up to the nurse's station.

"Hi there," I address the nurses.

I have returned to my room. My mom is wearing that look of pride, and surprise. The best way I can describe this look is if, for example, I had won the pornography equivalent of the Oscar. Sure, she'd be proud of me, but probably surprised none-the-less.

The folks who have been making the arrangements to get me the powered chair have returned, and learned of my left-side-only wheelchair mobility progress.

"The choice is yours. That can't be easy. Do you still want us to locate you a powered chair, or will that do?"

"No, thank you. This is fine, thanks," I state with no hesitation in the least.

Neither the first nor the last time I would take the harder path through this.

It is time to meet my roommates. It turns out the gentleman directly across from my bed, which, by-the-way, is closest to the bathroom, is leaving that same day. Good, don't need to give him a name. We'll just cast some drifter in the role when we shoot the movie version of this.

Next to the random guy-not-in-this-book is Roger. Roger is nearly eighty years old. Calling him a curmudgeon would be complimentary. He's an old codger, this guy. Roger broke his back some months ago when he fell off his roof. Why, you might ask, was Roger, a man of nearly eighty, on his roof? It would seem Roger is the strong, independent type. Roger was up on the roof adjusting his satellite dish. He missed his ladder on the way down. He is learning how to continue to be mobile, though his legs will never work again.

Roger is tough. Picture any "Old Man so-and-so" from *Scooby Doo*, "And I'd have gotten away with it too, if not for those lousy kids and their mangy mutt." That would be the type that best fits Roger.

To my right, my last roommate, Carter. Carter is a college professor, and a paraplegic. I never did learn how he lost the use of his legs, and in fact I think he had no use of anything below his waist, frankly. He was mostly quiet, but seemed to be your typical academic. The stoic, thoughtful, pipe-smoking blazer-wearing, buttoned-down, old-school type. We three could not be more diversely cast unless we were being put in an episode of *The Real World*.

OK...so where are the fucking cameras, anyhow?

Thus begins my next step in recovery. My mom is staying in town a few more days. Wants to be sure I am all settled in here before she heads home; Mom loves to worry. While I am safe at this point, my injuries are pretty grievous - and gross, too.

Twice a day the nurses come to clean my fixator. There are nine pins, of varying thickness, sticking out of different parts of my leg. At each point, skin and pin touch. These points need to be cleaned and sterilized rather frequently, so as to prevent infection.   If any of the above make you think, "Yuck", well, sorry…welcome to my world!

One of the first things they work with me on is the concept of transferring. No, this is not a reference to switching schools or changing buses at Albuquerque. When you have only one functional arm, and one functional leg, the business of moving from a bed, to a wheelchair, to bed again can be both an adventure, and potential danger. Falling would not be good. For starters, no clue how in the fuck I'd get back up. More than that, there are parts of my body falling onto would do me very little good. Then, just to add injury to insult, breaking any other bones and lessening my mobility will not be healthy for my recovery goals. But with the ability to transfer, I have gained yet another wonder. I can actually get to a toilet.

It's kind of surprising the stupid, mundane things we take so completely for granted. For example, I have always brushed my teeth with my right hand, and needed both hands to put contacts into, then take them out of, my eyes. When you have only one functional hand, things become complicated.

There are appropriate and inappropriate times to get up and go to the bathroom. Sitting at home, watching TV, you can get up and take a whiz or a dump at your convenience. Pushing past the row of fifteen in the middle of the best action scene during a movie is necessary sometimes, but slightly less appropriate, especially when you are causing popcorn to fly all over. But in either example, you can simply get up and go. When you can only bear weight on one leg, and only one arm is of any real use, it becomes difficult at best. Mind you, for weeks now, I have been peeing into a plastic bottle specifically designed for urine collection. I honestly don't think I pooped during my three weeks in the hospital. How odd.

Suddenly I have learned to move from the wheelchair to my bed, and back, and even from the wheelchair to a more mundane seat. Woo hoo! I think I might actually have shed a tear of joy the first time I had a seat upon the porcelain throne, and made a movement. Pathetic? Maybe. But you have no idea what it's like when this act is virtually impossible.

But again, I digress.

Very quickly I begin to learn to transfer myself with less and less effort. Further, due to my impatience, with less and less supervision. Initially, there must be a nurse, or PT, or OT, or some such present any time I move myself between venues. Fine, fine, but quickly I get impatient awaiting them. Hey, there are patients in this hospital with far greater needs than I. What I really hate is waiting to have someone watch me do something I need no actual help doing.

It turns out that is actually a good thing, on my part. Of course, the therapists want me to be able to do transfers unsupervised as soon as possible. That will be part of my recovery, and the sooner I am capable of it, the sooner I might get to go home to my cat. After some initial discouragement following my increasingly brazen transfers, it's decided that I am perfectly safe doing it all unsupervised. Yet again, I have managed to beat out their expectations. Go me!

I am well aware that doctors and therapists are big fans of being modest in their expectations. Nothing is more discouraging to a recovery than being told that your efforts are pointless, or that what you think might take days or weeks technically should take weeks or months. Granted, they cannot be too optimistic, either, lest they give false hope. Telling someone with severe nerve damage that they will make a complete recovery in time when they know as little as they do about the nervous system is unfair. And more, I don't think any two people with any kind of nerve damage recover the same. I have theories on that, but I'll save you from them, for now.

Thus far, I have been told it will be one to three years before I walk, and while I will likely recover full use of my arm, it could take years. These answers are not good enough. I will recover faster than that. Period. No arguments, no whining, no tears. I will make a much faster recovery than that.

I begin to get friendly with my nurses and therapists. I am, by my nature, a talker. If you've read this far, you get the gist. I am a people person. I love to tell a good joke, or a bad joke, or a terrible pun. I like to get to know the people around me, and interact as much as I can. I am a social animal in many senses of that term.

One other problem, which bothers me more that it probably should, is my voice.

There have been, thus far, two major surgeries. During my first, they tell me, I was under anesthetic for more than nine hours. As such, they intubated me. If you are unfamiliar with that technical term, it means they shoved a tube down my throat so I could breathe. Trouble is, upon extubation, or removal of the tube, they managed to scratch my vocal cords. The result left my voice pitched a good octave higher than normal, whispery and scratchy. Normally, I have a rather deep baritone. I was a DJ in college, and have had professional vocal training back in my high school days. While I stand at a whopping five foot six, my voice seems to stand more like six foot five.

Like all my other injuries, they have told me I will recover from that in time, too. It's a recurrent theme: You were hurt, you are suffering, now you must work on recovery.

Chapter 4 – Therapy isn't just for psychoanalysis.

Physical therapy occurs in two forms at Helen Hayes hospital. The first is group therapy, the second is individual time with a therapist. I have a nice, motherly woman, named Irene, as my therapist during the one-on-one sessions.

The group sessions for therapy often involve things that seem mundanely stupid, but it's amazing what serious injuries force, with regards to recovery. For example, standing.

It is something we just take for granted. Standing. You rise up, put the weight of your body on your feet, you straighten your back, and balance between the right and left. Easy, right? Well, sure - until you are broken. My right leg is, at this point, not weight bearing. Chances are, putting any serious pressure on it would be quite unpleasant. So I am certainly not going to be doing anything that might force me to put my foot down, so to speak.

One group therapy is to literally stand around a table. All of us partaking of this therapy, for various reasons, are not currently inclined to stand easily, or on both feet. There are a couple of older women from the other side of the ward in this group. In fact, it should be noted that, with one exception, I am the youngest person in my ward. By a lot. There is, however, the one exception. A kid by the name of Allen. Allen is eighteen. Allen is a freshman in college. Allen likes to party. Allen was doing heavy drinking on a rooftop somewhere. Allen was goofing off, and tripped himself up, and fell onto and then through a skylight. Allen is more broken than I am.

Thus, the poor kid shattered his pelvis. And the damage is such that, at least for the time being, he has a colostomy bag. It is hoped that, as he recovers, that will be something that can be corrected. Still, he is a very unfortunate kid. He has high spirits at the time, though. As per Allen's suggestion, most of the time spent standing around this table is done playing Uno. Many, many games of Uno are played. Some of us can stand longer than others. Yes, I am only standing on my left leg for twenty minutes at a time, but some of the other elderly folk here can only manage five minutes or so before they need to retake their seats. Allen, it seems, is a bit competitive; he likes a challenge. I later learned that the therapists loved that I caused him to work harder.

Physical therapy, or PT, was for my legs. Occupational therapy, or OT, was for my arms and hands and such. Like PT, OT consisted of both group and individual sessions. The group sessions involved exercises with light weights, and were again a mix of folks. Allen was still with me, along with Carter from my room. Additionally, there was a gentleman by the name of Bruce. Bruce was in his mid-thirties, and a believer in whatever Christian faith he held. A deep believer, but despite his zealousness, he was accepting of other belief systems, and never tried to push or convert or persuade anyone else to his ways.

Bruce had been living a decent, stand-up life, and he had been with his family, and swimming. Bruce decided to show off, and dive into the pool. You know how they warn you to never dive into a pool that is too shallow? Bruce apparently neglected to heed that warning – and broke his neck. Bruce was a quadriplegic, technically. However, through faith and hard work, and an apparently iron will, Bruce was regaining the use of his arms and hands. That was very inspiring to me. I am finding that I am spending time outside my room with both Bruce and Carter, and occasionally Allen. Somehow, the four of us have bonded.

Bruce and Carter have been here together previously. I am closest in age to Allen, even though I am almost ten years older, and Bruce is next closest to me in age, within about ten years or so.

As I mentioned, my roommates, Carter and Roger, and I, were in a room meant for four. Early on the second or third morning I was at Helen Hayes, they brought us a fourth. Felix was eighty-five. He had just had his hip replaced. He was still pretty heavily drugged up. Truth was, Felix probably did not belong in rehab with us for at least another week or so. Felix cried and whined a lot. It's both disturbing and saddening at the same time.

Almost worse than Felix, however, is his wife. She seems like a nice enough lady, but she is in our room with Felix every morning by eight am. Now, really, we don't have many good reasons to be up before nine, but as soon as she arrives, Felix begins to cry piteously, and he is noisy. On top of that, mind you, this is now a room of three older men, and me, and they all snore - and not in unison. There are three very distinct, disturbing, loud snores. Suffice it to say, in addition to my usual nightly cocktail of drugs, we've added a sleep aid. It's that, or I am never sleeping.

I have now mentioned my daily drug cocktails, which I receive twice a day, in fact. Due to the severe and numerous injuries I have incurred, they have me on three rather strong pain meds. Oxycontin and Percocet are known narcotics. In fact, my doctor had wanted to move me to Vikadin instead of Percocet, but that presented a problem. Vikadin, if you do not know, is a codeine derivative.

Long ago, when I was home from college on a winter break, I came down with a truly nasty flu bug. Made me absolutely miserable. My doctor prescribed Tylenol three with codeine. I took it - and proceeded to break out in a rash. My mom has worked in the medical field in one capacity or another for a long, long time now. She suspected that rash was not from the flu, but was a reaction to the codeine. Great. Wonderful. Thus I have one known allergy.

In addition to Oxycontin and Percocet, I am also being given Neurontin. The latter is a neuropathic pain inhibitor. Considering the severity of the nerve damage to my arm, it is a necessity.

Anyone who knows me knows that I hate taking drugs. For any reason. I take Advil only if I am in pain to the point of impaired function. I begrudgingly take decongestants when I can only sniffle through my nose. It almost took an army of friends, led by Torrance, to get me to start taking Claritin regularly for my constant snuffling during heavy allergy seasons. As such, I wanted to wean myself off these meds as soon as I could, especially the narcotics. Since I was less certain of what, exactly, the Neurontin was doing, I tried to go without that first.

The nurse, as per usual, came one morning with my cocktail of drugs: The itty-bitty Oxycontin, the almost horse-pill sized Percocet, and the yellow capsule, Neurontin. Mmmmmmmmm, chalky.

"I think today I want to try to go without the Neurontin," I tell her.

"Are you sure?"

"Yeah, I think so."

"Ok. Well we'll keep it at the station for you, just in case."

"Thank you." My bold and daring plan to get off some of these nasty drugs lasted a whole and total two hours. It took slightly less time than that before I learned just what the Neurontin was doing.

The nerve damage in my arm was causing the nerves to fire their synaptic signals as per usual, but sans any connections. So, rather than twist my wrist, or bend my arm at the elbow, they just randomly fired. That, I learned, was why I was in almost a constant, dull pain. Dull being the key word. The Neurontin, it seems, kept that pain dull, as opposed to sharp. Dull was annoying. Sharp was agonizing. The nurses were very sympathetic when I rolled up in my wheelchair and asked for my Neurontin dose.

The rehab hospital was very different from the regular one. It was a bit more open, spatially, and of course fewer people on the verge of death. There were lots of broken people, which was what brought us all there, but not so much with the death and dying. And like the regular hospital…the food was nothing to write home about. Unless, of course, you were writing home and asking them to send better food!

Like all things, learning to maneuver a fork left handed took a bit more effort. Spoons were easier. Using a combination of a fork and knife would take a bit longer. By my second week there, I had regained enough use of the fingers on my right hand to do something more with it.

I discovered, not long after my arrival, that there were some options for food beyond the standard menu. Still bland, but at least less boring than the normal culinary experience. Worse than that, though, normally we would eat in our hospital rooms. In the real world, eating in one's bedroom is not a normal occurrence. What's more, between Roger griping about this pain or that and rambling on, or Felix's crying constantly, working up anything verging on an appetite was somewhat of a challenge. Thus Carter, Bruce and I often took to an unused dining room to partake of our meals, occasionally joined by Allen. Better company, less disquiet.

It took, maybe, a grand total of three days for me to become completely sick of the food offerings from the kitchens of Helen Hayes. Fortunately, my nurses were very sympathetic, and made the "mistake" of showing me the menu for a Chinese restaurant that would deliver. The first such meal, my mom graciously picked up the tab for. After a month of hospital food, punctuated only by a turkey club mom and my stepdad had brought to the previous hospital, an egg roll was a culinary masterpiece.

I want to take this moment, should she ever read this story, to thank my mom. She was really there for me, and she spent weeks in a place I know she is not overly fond of, in order to help care for me. That also meant my cat had some company, which was not a bad thing.

My mom and I get along well, for the most part, but she can be a bit overbearing sometimes. She means well, but she sometimes does not realize who I am, compared to who she believes I should be. At any rate, mom had been in New York for almost a month, and needed to go back to work, and go home to her husband and her dog. I was okay with that. She was tearful, but then, getting my mom to tears is not too different from shooting fish in a barrel, and takes very little effort. Soon my dad took her to the airport, and she returned to her life in Chicago.

In addition to the rehabilitation activities occurring daily, I had guests stopping by to visit, and had been brought several very useful toys. My cell phone, which I could use in most parts of the hospital, a CD Walkman and some discs from my car, and more than that, my ancient laptop PC. I was able to connect to the internet, for the first time in nearly a month, and catch up with people all around me I seldom see in person. Now I had an outlet, late at night, that would not disturb my already disturbed roommates, and I could keep my mind somewhat intact.

In-as-much as my mind was ever intact, which brings me to a good point to get into some issues with regards to the women in my life, and my relationships.

Chapter 5 – Relationship fu one-oh-one.

This part gets sticky. Now is a good time to take a break, get some popcorn and a soda, and enjoy the edgy, gossipy Warren-the-womanizer section of the story. Our hero, you see, is flawed.

I suck at relationships; it's as simple as that. I am indecisive, uncommunicative, and unfaithful. I don't tell lies, per se, usually. I omit details on occasion. I am sometimes rather mercurial and aloof with regards to my relationships, and learned, over the years, valuable lessons in how not to be a total fuck-up. I'm not a user, not abusive, just not much of a lover. Mind you, it's only now, as I retell my tale, that I can observe myself in this manner. I had a very different perspective at the time of this situation, and a very different understanding of my own mindset, back when all this was going on.

Torrance and I had been, as mentioned before, on again, off again, etc. We would date - then not date. But we'd be sleeping together. And then dating. Then not. Still having sex. Beyond the sex, there were many ups and downs in our bizarre relationship. I loved her, well, to be perfectly fair, I had no idea what it was I felt for her - didn't know it was love until much, much later, but we'll get to that further along in this story. When I was first brought to the hospital, it was apparently Tori whom I was asking for. Loving, no?

Then there was Jillian. Jill was eighteen. I was twenty-seven. When we met, Jillian was almost sixteen, and though underage, we would flirt. Nothing behind it, just flirting. Jill, along with Bob's girlfriend Sheila and their friend Lori, became my cheerleaders. I had my own fencing cheerleaders, yeah. They thought it was fun and cute, and I was certainly amused by it. They referred to themselves as my fencer groupies.

Not long after Jill turned eighteen, we were alone together doing something or other; I cannot recall now. Flirting occurred, which led to kissing.

To be fair, when this began, Tori and I were in an off-again period. Of course, off-again but still sleeping together.

Jillian was young, and inexperienced; we took it slow. Over time kissing lead to petting which lead to oral. Then, one afternoon, I took her virginity. Sex between us became a semi-regular occurrence. It had to be totally discreet; no one could know. And of course, during that time, Tori and I hit an on-again phase - then off-again. So, I was sleeping with Tori semi-regularly, and also with Jill from time to time.

Yes, I am a bad man. Thanks for playing.

No one suspected anything. No one knew anything. And I thought Jillian would keep it all together, and under her hat.

My near-death unhinged her, I guess. One afternoon, Tori came to the rehab hospital. Damn was she angry.

"We need to talk. In private."

"Okay."

We found an unused room.

"What's up?"

"Have you been sleeping with Jillian?"

My heart skipped a beat. I could not stop myself.

"No, baby, why would you ask that?"

"Because she told me."

Heart skips another beat. "She told you what?"

"She told me you two have been sleeping together for months."

The lie escaped my lips as easily as if it were true. "No, sweetie, that's not true. When would I have had the time?"

"If it's not true, why would she be saying it to me?"

I have no idea how I conjured this one so instantaneously, but I knew, to the core of my being, that I would lose Tori completely if I came clean.

"Maybe because, well, you know she has a thing for me. Maybe she wishes it were so, and made it so real in her mind that she confessed to you, hoping that you would be able to bond over me, somehow."

No, Tori is not stupid, and she would never have bought it - had Jillian, realizing what she had done, not confessed that, yes, she made it all up in her head.

Love makes us all do crazy things. I realized, long after all this happened, that I had loved two very different women, in two different ways.

Skipping ahead a bit, even though she bought the story, Tori still opted to go ahead and travel with her family to celebrate the New Year. They had been planning on a cruise with her grandmother for months, and after my accident she had decided she'd stay here with me. However, even though Jill had confirmed to her satisfaction that there was not, in fact, anything between us, Tori determined that she'd get away for a bit, and take the cruise. That turned out to be a good thing. During the cruise, Tori's grandmother collapsed several hours before midnight. She was aware of the time, somehow, and apparently wished the family a happy new year around midnight. She died a few hours later, but had managed, as she had wanted, to survive to the start of the twenty-first century. She died surrounded by her whole family, and the love that represented. But I digress.

I have never been an enormous fan of the holidays, for a number of reasons. Growing up in the Midwest, and being Jewish, I always wound up feeling kind of shunned by the whole Christmas thing. The number of Jews in the Chicagoland area are far, far smaller than New York. Then there is the commercialization. The music begins to get played around Thanksgiving, and often doesn't stop until New Year's. Now, c'mon, I am all for tunes to get into the holiday spirit, but it gets to be a little much after a while.

Don't think me a Grinch or Scrooge, though I will toss out the occasional "humbug," "Bah, holidays!" Yet I have always loved *Rudolph the Rednosed Reindeer*, and *Frosty the Snowman*, and *It's Christmas Charlie Brown* and the pathetic, half-dead tree and Linus' speech about the spirit, and blah blah blah. Over the years I've grown more cynical about the entire affair, and how much it has gotten away from the "peace-on-earth good will towards men" attitude, and more to shop and buy and give and give and give, and max out your credit cards. So, yes, just a tad jaded about it all.

Anyhow, here I am, trapped in a rehabilitation hospital, and the only radio station they can tune into at the nurses' station is playing Xmas music, and that's it. Endless Christmas music, all day, every day. The door to my room is approximately two feet from the offending stereo.

You can only hear Paul McCartney's *Simply Having a Wonderful Christmas Time* so many times before the urge to commit a brutal murder begins to come over you.

I plotted my revenge. Oh yes, I had it all planned out. There would be no stopping me. The radio had a CD player in it, and was at the top of wheelchair reachable height. I would stealthily roll up to the CD player, calmly, quietly drop in the disc. No one would see, no one would notice. Then I would hit play…and roll away will all of my might, left arm pumping for dear life.

Then the dulcet tones of Nine Inch Nails' *Wish* would overtake the floor. I'd feel better. Some of the nurses, not far in age from me, might even have enjoyed the momentary break. But the old folks that made up the vast majority of this ward would have run me down, and rolled over me with my own wheelchair, I don't doubt.

A man can dream - and without a Christmas music soundtrack in the background, too. The incessant music slowly began to make me crazy, and going crazy in the midst of the level of insanity I was already surrounded by was not going to bode well.

Dad and Lucy stopped in to visit a couple times a week. Dad and I had not been so close when I was growing up, since he'd left about the time I was ten or so, and my sister was even younger. Once I moved local to him, we actually began to develop a relationship. As such, all throughout this ordeal, he has been there for me.

A lot of friends stopped by and visited. Bob and Sheila would pop in from time to time and say, "Hi." I even managed to get them to bring our choir in for a practice, one Monday evening. Not a huge chorus, but we did have a fun evening, and my dad even provided an extra bass line. I was not much of a bass at that point – still just kinda had that scratchy, throaty, wispy high voice. My old friend Randall and his girlfriend Leanne made a point of stopping in en route from South Jersey to her family's place in Massachusetts. Randall got me into the SCA back in college, and it's always good to see him. Leanne has been a friend quite a while now, too. They brought me a set of pictures that were taken at Pennsic last year.

Wow. Pennsic. Every August, over ten thousand people invade and take over a camp site in southwest Pennsylvania. It's pretty amazing, really. A lot of great fun, many medieval activities including archery, fencing, feasting, dancing, drumming, heavy combat, many classes, and parties every night. As William, I attend it annually, and always come away with incredible stories. I almost always come home far more relaxed than I departed.

Pennsic is over eight months away, but I can't help but wonder if I will even be standing by August. Let alone fencing. Not something to think about at this time.

Of course, Jillian visited me.

"I'm sorry, sweetie, but why did you have to do that?" I ask. It's a lame excuse for a pseudo-apology.

"I don't know," she admits quietly. "I just thought maybe it would bring us closer. I just didn't think."

"No, you didn't," I admonished her. Mr. Sensitive, I was. "This put me in a really awkward position."

"I know," she states.

Wow was I being a schmuck.

Of course, everyone believed now that Jill was, in fact, nuts, and so they were not being very kind to her. While I was defending her, taking the time to point out her youth and inexperience in relationships and so on, my turning on her like that had not been helpful. But she loved me, and for me and my reputation, she would let her own be ruined.

Go ahead, say it. You know you want to. You're thinking it.

Asshole.

Yup.

We were moving along a quieter hallway of the hospital, and came upon an open door. The room was dark, and Jill went to take a peek inside.

Jillian can be cute, and motioned me in. She closed the door, and climbed onto my lap, and began to kiss me. I will leave the rest up to your imagination.

Chapter 6 – Testing…testing. Is this thing on?

In addition to all the therapy and such, there were constant visits with doctor types. I think every few days they x-rayed my leg and shoulder. I wish I had collected that stuff for future viewing. Then, one day, they performed a test called an EMG.

EMG is the abbreviation used for Electromyography. The test involves two parts, both of which would go over fantastically in Iraq for the torturing of prisoners of war. The first involves electrodes, which are attached at various points. For me, it was the right arm and right leg, at different intervals. Then, current is run through those electrodes to test the nerve responses.

It should be mentioned that the current is altered, increased even, depending on how one reacts. There was at least one point that the jolt to my leg caused me to kick with the other, good leg.

Then, the jolts to my arm, usually an annoyance over my normal situation, was occasionally excruciating. And of course, EMG readings are open to interpretation. What did we learn? We learned that while the nerve damage is severe, it is not, apparently, permanent. How long will it take to recover? God only knows. And he isn't talking. The powers-that-be have such a sense of humor.

Oh, I should also mention the *other* part of the EMG test. A needle is inserted into a muscle, then moved around, causing a sensation that can only be described as unpleasant. Try sticking a needle into your bicep; then, for kicks, shift it about some. Dig a bit while you're at it. Hook it up to a small battery for a slight jolt. Sound thoroughly unpleasant? Well, yes, it is. Don't try this at home. If I never have another EMG performed again, it will be too soon.

Chapter 7 – Turn of the Century – what if the Y-two-kay bug brings us to the end?

New Years' Eve was approaching, and I had no intent on staying in the hospital. I'd already been here for Christmas.

"There's a party. I have a friend who will come to get me. I would really like to go."

After consultation between the doctors, nurses, and my therapists, they gave me permission. New Year's Eve came, and my friend Deb did, in fact, come to get me. In the SCA, they call Deb by the name Kayleigh. She and I shoot archery together, and we are both in the choir.

Oh, and I suppose I should mention that, while she's a nice looking lady, I don't actually find Deb attractive. See, it's not *all* females! Anyhow, she showed up, and wheeled me out to her truck. I had on my tux shirt and jacket, and those odd basketball pants that button up the side. Having that monster fixator attached to my leg limited my clothing options quite a bit. Because of it, I could wear no shoe, so I had put a flannel pillow case over my foot to keep it warm.

We rolled along, chit-chatting. This was my first venture away from a hospital, and not in an ambulance, in over a month. To get to the party, it was necessary to pass by my neighborhood. As we passed along the street, approaching the post office, I pressed my face to the window.

"What are you doing?" Deb asked me.

"I'm looking to see if I can find any pieces of my tibia out there."

I certainly thought I was funny.

We got to Chris' party some twenty minutes later.

Chris is about twenty years my senior, exactly, as we share a birthday. Chris is a professional photographer, and dabbler in the stock market. As each of us came in, he took a photo. There I was, in my glasses, tux shirt and coat, and black fingerless gloves to better grip the wheels of the chair, and I know that, somewhere, I still have that photo.

It was a good party. A lot of friends were there, several of whom I had not seen since before the accident. My leg was a source of both fascination and loathing, as it was not by any stretch of the imagination pretty. The monstrous skin graft in particular is just not pretty to look at, especially when I flex in any way, and it moves. But it felt good to be doted on, and good to not be in a hospital environment. Tears came to my eyes more than once that night.

Midnight struck, and I only took a small sip of champagne. I was still on a very heavy pain medication regimen. In the blink of an eye, the twenty first century began, and the toasters and other computerized electronics of the world neither self-destructed, nor attacked, as the "Y2K" doom-sayers had been predicting.

I had been told to be back at the hospital by midnight. Now, of course, they knew I'd be late, but we couldn't stay out till two am. Deb drove me back, and I was sad to be returning. Who knew how much longer I'd have to be there?

That question was weighing heavily on my mind. Between the holidays, and the weekends, there were a number of times when there was no therapy to be had. I felt that being in a rehab hospital and not receiving any therapy was a colossal waste of time and, even though I figured insurance was covering it, money. So I pushed, and pushed hard.

My occupational therapist felt that we had done much, and that, if I continued to work on my own, and with the in-home therapists that would be sent, I would continue to regain use of the muscles in my arm. My hand was mostly working, even though my thumb, index finger and middle finger remained largely numb. My arm, though devoid of sensitivity at various points, was beginning to work. I had regained some strength in my shoulder and triceps.

Of course, there was still no bearing weight on my right leg. That presented several problems my physical therapist continued to address. They wanted me to get vertical as often as possible. Using crutches was out; my arm was still too weak to support my weight, since I could only balance on my left leg. And even a walker posed problems, since, again, one leg worked, and I could really only use one arm.

The solution was an interesting one. They concocted a walker with a brace for my right arm, which could be strapped down by my left using Velcro, while I would lean, placing the weight at my more functional shoulder and triceps. Then, with a sort of shuffle, I could move the walker forward, and hop on my left leg. Move forward, hop. Move forward, hop. It was an odd and bizarre motion, but it worked, and it returned some of my mobility. One large issue, however, was my home itself. I was living in a second story apartment, with no elevator.

The railing up was on the left side of the staircase, and there was no other on the wall on the right, so balancing and hopping would not work. I could not drag the leg with the fixator attached; chances are, I'd jar something loose, and that would be most uncomfortable.

I actually came up with the solution myself. If I could keep my right leg elevated, while going up the stairs on my butt, using my left arm and left leg to pull/push, I should be able to ascend the stairs. At the bottom, I could transfer from the wheelchair to the lowest stoop. At the top, I'd use a chair to regain level, and then transfer to the wheelchair, once someone had gotten it up. That, of course, meant that without assistance, I was not leaving my apartment. I figured, and may have even stated, in an emergency, I would push the wheelchair down the stairs, and work my way down. It was crazy, sure, but it would let me go home. If it worked. Of course, it would need to be tested.

So, we went to a stairwell in the hospital, and I put the brakes on and climbed out of my wheelchair. I lowered myself to the lowest stoop, using only my left arm and left leg. Then, carefully, I ascended the staircase on my ass. At the top, my therapist had provided a chair. As predicted, I easily transferred to it from the top stoop. Okay, halfway there. I have made it up the stairs. So, how is down going to work? Reversing the process, we learned that down was no harder.

"Well, Warren, you've done it. Tomorrow is Friday. You want us to release you Monday?"

"Any therapy Saturday or Sunday?"

"No."

"Then how about letting me go home tomorrow."

"Well, okay."

Torrance had returned home from her cruise, but fate loves to toy with her as much as it does with me. Even after the trauma of losing her grandmother, there was a surprise in store for her.

"Yeah, so, my car is gone."

"What?"

"Well, I left it outside of my sister's house, came back, and - it was gone."

"Someone stole the damned Jeep?"

"Yup."

"That sucks."

"Yes it does."

Fortunately, I was not able to drive my car, and Tori had no trouble with the manual transmission. I let her take my car till she found her own, or acquired a new one.

I was excited to tell her the good news.

"I am going home tomorrow."

"Want me to be there?"

"Please."

Chapter 8 – Homecoming. Does my cat remember me?

It was a big to-do. My dad and stepmom came to get me. I said farewell to my roommates, and Bruce, Allen, and Carter in particular. I thanked my therapists for all their hard work. I said good-bye to my nurses. Then my wheelchair was loaded into the trunk, I was loaded into the car, and we departed from Helen Hayes hospital.

I was beyond thrilled by the prospect of going home. It had been so long now; I was so ready. I missed my bed, my things, my personal space. I just wanted to be home.

There would still be some logistical problems. My bathroom was on the far side of the apartment from the bedroom, so moving across the place would not always be easy. As such, they'd provided me with one of those plastic jars to pee in. Not pretty, but better than pissing myself in the middle of the night. The wheelchair would not fit into the bedroom door. For some reason, it was much narrower than any other. Well, OK, fine, so I set up the walker for my room. I would only be in there on the computer or going to bed anyhow, so transferring to a chair or the bed most of the time.

I was beyond happy when we drove into the parking area at the back of my apartment.

It was a two story house, very old, that had been turned into apartments long ago. Four, to be precise, with two on each floor. Mine was the largest, and had the most closet space. I had, at this point, lived in the building longest, too.

My father rolled me to the door and into the hallway. At the bottom of the stairs, I rose up on my left leg, left hand on the railing. Dad took the wheelchair up, and Torrance had placed the chair at the top of the stairs. I slowly dropped to my butt, and up the stairs I went. I transferred from the chair to my wheelchair, and rolled into my over-sized kitchen. God, did I miss that place.

"Shira, I am home!" I called to my cat.

She peaked around the corner a moment, meowed and ran off. It seemed that she was pissed at me for having been away - and the wheelchair scared her.

I started to cry.

Soon I was settled in, and dad and Lucy, who had brought dinner and cookies, were gone, leaving Tori and Shira and me alone.

"How's it feel to be home?"

"I can't describe it. I missed this place."

"I filled your humidifier. Shira has been fed. Will you be okay?"

"I think so. Thanks, sweetie."

Damn was that woman good to me. I know, prior statement - asshole. Thank you, I know.

Tori took her leave, and I relished being home for the first time in six weeks. I climbed into bed later, and wow, was it larger and more comfortable than the hospital beds had been. I had the extra pillow for my poor right leg, because the fixator was forcing me still to sleep on my back. Never been a back sleeper; I have normally slept on my belly. That situation would not make sleep easy, by any stretch of the imagination.

As I began to doze, finally, Shira leapt onto my bed. My little calico-love nuzzled my cheek, and began to purr; I reached out with my left hand and stroked between her ears, and cried. I was home.

Chapter 9 – Ask not for whom the phone rings.

The phone rang about six fifteen am.

"H-hello?"

"Hi, Mr. Mushnik? This is Allie, the visiting nurse?"

"Y-yeah? What do you want?"

"I will be coming over in about an hour and a half to clean your wounds. Just wanted to let you know."

"Yeah, sure, thanks."

I was groggy, and no way was I getting back to sleep.

Allie was a lovely girl, probably a year or two younger than I. She was working for the nursing group from the local hospital, on an exchange program of some sort, since the local nurses were on strike. Her accent told me she was from Georgia.

Allie checked my blood pressure, which I had learned over the past six weeks was pretty much always one-ten over seventy or eighty. Yes, while I was short and fat, my blood pressure was dead even. To this day, nearly every visit to the doctor, for any reason, results in at least two checks on my blood pressure. I always find it annoying that the doctors seem to expect something else.

Allie then proceeded to clean the pins. It was a simple, but kind of icky procedure. Allie would use a long q-tip, which was dipped in a special solution, to clean the skin surrounding the base of the pins. It was sometimes tender, but she used a gentle touch. She would then swab it with a gel. Lastly, she applied a special cream to my skin graft, then packed her things and was off.

My days that first week were spent getting used to getting around my apartment, getting re-acquainted with my cat, and making myself at home again. My original doctor wanted to do a follow-up, dad told me, and it was scheduled for the following Monday.

The coming weekend was an SCA event on Long Island, and Torrance was coming to take me, Saturday.

Tuesday morning the phone rang again about six thirty.

"H-hello?"

"Hi there, Mr. Mushnik? This is Allie, the visiting nurse. I will be there in about an hour, okay?"

"Yeah, okay."

Rinse. Repeat.

Wednesday, six twenty am.

"Hello?"

"Mr. Mushnik? This is Allie, the visiting nurse."

Rinse, repeat. Again.

Thursday, six thirty am.

"Mr. Mushnik? This is Allie, the visiting nurse."

Once more with feeling.

Friday, six am.

"Mr. Mushnik? This is Allie, the visiting nurse."

Yes, fine. I am used to you now, Allie. Is it really necessary for you to call me so fucking early when you are still an hour or more away, and I have nowhere I need to be during the day?

Somewhere around Wednesday, my voice returned to normal. I just woke up, coughed once, and suddenly I could talk like myself. The baritone tone I was so accustomed to had come back, just like that. My guess has always been that the humidifier constantly running had been what had allowed it, at last. Hospitals are notoriously dry.

Saturday Tori picked me up and we went to the SCA event on Long Island. It was odd to be in garb, and in a wheelchair. People were really pleased to see me.

"William, damn, it is so good to see you alive and well!"

"I am so glad you're doing well, Will."

"Wow, Will, I can't believe you're here!"

And so on. It felt good to be seen. Yeah, it was a bit awkward, and I was often being pushed by Tori, or Bob, or Sheila, or Deb, but I was at an event, and it felt good to be social.

Our choir sang that afternoon at court, since our director was receiving an award from the King and Queen. That was pretty cool.

It was decided we should all go out for dinner. There was a Chinese restaurant suggested that was nearby. We packed ourselves up, Tori and I in my car, since hers was still missing, and the group of us went to dinner.

Trouble was, the only way into the restaurant was by stairs. Not very many, but they were there. I was feeling bold. I was feeling strong. I opted to hop down those stairs on my good leg, supporting myself with my left arm on the railing. They were cold and damp, so I did not relish going down them on my tush.

I am a moron.

My leg or arm gave out; I couldn't tell you which, and my fixator impacted upon the cement stairs.

Tori claims the sound I made was perhaps one of the most terrifying things she has ever heard. Once the shock and pain wore down, and the tears stopped, I managed to finish descending the last couple of stairs. I climbed into my wheelchair, and rolled into the restaurant proper. I seemed to be okay. There was blood around one of the pins, but nothing was loose. I was very glad now that I'd be seeing my doctor on Monday.

I managed to enjoy dinner, even though I was achy. Tori bundled me up, then Bob and our friend Dave lifted me and the chair up the stairs, taking no chances.

We made it home, and I cleaned the area that had bled, around the pin. Tori stayed that night, which was a comfort, though a bit uncomfortable. Tori cleaned the pins in my leg Sunday morning. But I was more and more certain that this was something I was now quite capable of managing on my own.

Monday morning, six am. Can you guess what's about to happen?

"Good morning, Mr. Mushnik? This is Allie, the visiting nurse."

Here we go again.

Chapter 10 – Let's talk about semantics, shall we?

Monday dad and Lucy came to get me, and we trekked into the city for what would be my first follow-up exam by Doctor Weiss. I am very fortunate to have him; he's one of the best in the field. I am nervous to tell him about the fall, but it will have to be done.

We get to his office, and he takes a quick look at me, then sends me to be x-rayed.

At this point, I think they've x-rayed me a good dozen times. I'm starting to think my leg is going to glow in the dark soon. The tech comes in, gives me the usual lead smock, and shoots my leg, then my shoulder.

I remained there for a bit, long enough for my film to be developed.

"Damn," the tech states. "That is the most broken leg I have ever seen."

Thanks a lot

"Yeah, it's a doozy," I say.

We return to Doctor Weiss' office, and the x-rays are up on the screen. You can see the pins sticking in--not pretty--and from the ankle up, the remains of my tibia, like an open flower--clearly wrecked. My fibula is obviously broken in two places. Apparently, that is what the fixator is holding together. The x-ray of my shoulder has me puzzled. There is something not right, something solid in the picture, with ridges along the top. Did they get something into the shot?

Doctor Weiss comes in, and checks the x-rays.

"Ummm, well, the leg is healing, some," he says quietly, moving to the x-ray of my shoulder, "The plates look pretty good."

"Plates? What plates?" I ask, confused.

He doesn't turn to me, he's still examining the x-ray, "We had to put three titanium plates into your shoulder to repair your shattered clavicle."

"Wait a minute. What do you mean shattered? I was told it was fractured!"

"No, it was shattered."

"There is a big difference between fractured and shattered!"

It seems I was the only one who thought so. Great, so now I know that I have three titanium plates holding my clavicle together. Seven weeks in, and now I learn this. And just for kicks, I realize I can feel the plates under the skin and scar tissue.

Adventures in visiting the doctor. On the plus side, I did no damage when I fell onto the fixator that night. That is good news. I have enough damage at this point as it is; I don't need more.

Arrangements are discussed so we won't be returning to New York City to visit Dr. Weiss. He does some office hours in Rockland, so we'll go see him there. That is far more convenient to my home.

Tuesday morning, six thirty am.

Join in the chorus, please.

"Hi, Mr. Mushnik? This is Allie, the visiting nurse…"

Oh-for-the-love-of-God, don't you think I know who you are by now? Why, oh why do you continue to assist in wrecking my already terrible sleep?

Somewhere in here we begin the visits from my new in-home therapists. A couple times a week, a physical therapist (PT) and an occupational therapist (OT) will be stopping by my house. Eventually, when they remove the fixator, I will go back to Helen Hayes for outpatient therapy. This does, of course, presume I might be able to drive again, but we'll burn that bridge when we come to it. So at any rate, there will be a pair of therapists coming by, and helping me to continue to improve, as much as we can, to arrest the already existent muscle atrophy, and prevent any further. Sounds like a plan to me.

I was given tools and exercises, before I left the hospital, to continue on my own to improve, and I use them multiple times a day. If I am going to grab this bull by its horns and recover as quickly as I can, I will do everything in my power to make it happen! I use a foamy, Nerf-esque ball to work my arms, and flat, stretchy, rubbery bands for both my arms and legs. I get vertical as much as I can. I work on being as mobile as I can. I will not take any of this lying down. Or, for that matter, sitting in a wheelchair too long.

My physical therapist is a thin, brunette, motherly type. She is personable enough, and has a good attitude. She likes that I want to work, and that's what we do. She pushes me as far as she can, and I like that she wants to push as much as I do. She comes in, does her thing, and when she leaves I have made improvements and learned something new to continue to maintain the strength in my legs as best I can.

My occupational therapist, on the other hand, is not very helpful. She is a lithe unattractive blonde woman who comes in, does stupid little tasks with me that I am already beyond when she starts, and leaves after fifteen to twenty minutes. An example: one day she comes in with a little peg board thing, and tiny plastic pegs. The mission? Pick up tiny pegs, insert them into the peg board, repeat.

Now, okay, yes, good, fine motor control in the fingers is important; but I am already using my right hand as often as possible, have been since before I left rehab. This is something I was capable of two weeks ago already, and continue to, more-or-less, practice on my own. On top of that, this was the extent of her fifteen minute visit. I refer to my OT, with no affection, as Dippy Dolittle. An aptly descriptive title for that rather useless, dizzy blonde woman.

A moment to comment--speaking my mind here-- had she been a ditzy brunette or redhead, the title would have been unchanged. She was dippy, and did nothing. I like blondes, despite the wealth of jokes about their occasional foibles with regards to overall intelligence. So don't read this as some lame reflection of a poor attitude on my part toward blonde women. Thank you.

This has been a public service announcement from the broken and annoyed. We now return you to your story.

Wednesday morning, seven am - yup, made it to seven this time.

"Mr. Mushnik? Yes, this is Allie, the visiting nurse..."

Insert witty remark of annoyance here.

This just never gets old. No, wait. Yes it does. It gets old really fast.

Chapter 11 – Travelogue of the handicapped.

Wednesday night has always been fencing practice. Well, one of them, at any rate. And I really would like to go, if I could drive, or fence, or even depart my home of my own free will. No dice.

Tori and I made a trip to the mall. That proved to be an adventure on many levels. For starters, I now understand why handicapped parking is how it is. I have been issued a temporary handicapped permit. This lovely red plastic piece is to be hung from the rearview mirror of whatever vehicle I am being transported in, and will not expire til October, Ten months from now. Oy.

Anyhow, it allows me to be parked in those lovely blue parking spots. To all the assholes out there who park in handicapped spaces, but are not themselves handicapped, be it for any amount of time at all: You suck. Not only is that space rather limited, but it is also not often as useful as advertised. I don't care how extra wide a space may be, morons behind the wheel of any vehicle can't necessarily park. And on top of that, in the dead of winter, having to transfer from a warm car to a lukewarm wheelchair in the bloody cold is not a whole lot of fun. Brrrrr.

So in addition to the joys of handicapped parking, there is also the thrill of the various doors into any place. Sure, great, fine, you can hit a button, and like some monstrous gate into Hades, the great glass and steel doors swing open at a speed that leads me to believe it might be Halloween by the time I can wheel into the mall. Then, to add to the fun, there is that lovely saddle between the door frames. I mean, seriously, if you go and make something handicapped accessible, why the fuck do you throw in something the equivalent of a speed bump at the point of entry?

Of course, as soon as teenagers see the double doors open of their own accord, like some kind of very lame *Star Trek* effect, they crowd around you. Thanks, kids. Really. Just ignore the cripple in the wheelchair. People can be so rude sometimes.

So now we get to roll into the mall. Woo, hoo. The great American landmark cluster-fuck that is the shopper's paradise, the mall. Of course, any venture from home is a welcome departure from staring at those same four walls. We are planning to go and see a movie, since this particular mall has a theater.

Sizes of malls do not impress me nearly as much as architecture and shopping opportunities. Today, we are visiting the Palisades Mall in West Nyack, New York. This mall was once slated to be the second largest in the nation, but due to protestation on the part of the local township and other factors, it is barely in the top twenty for size. This mall is four floors, with underground parking below. There are a bunch of interesting quirks about it, though.

The Palisades Mall was built on ground that is the combination of a small mountain, and a landfill. As such, I was once told that the parking garage should have had concrete poured before asphalt was laid down. The management company of the mall decided that was a waste; they'd just patch the holes that might occur. I doubt, highly, they anticipated those holes being large enough to eat a car, forcing closure of the garage so they might be repaired, every few months. Further, one of the parking structures is, in fact, built around a cemetery. No, seriously, people's long-dead relatives are interred just off the ramp of the garage. I somehow doubt this is good karma for the mall and its owners.

Additionally, this mall is terribly ugly. They were clearly going for some kind of post-modern ultra-cool industrial look, and in the small scale foam-core model they probably built first, it looked really neat. Then they blew it up to life size – or, rather, larger-than-life size. Nope, they didn't hit this building with an ugly stick. They beat the ever-loving crap out of it. Big faux-trees with inverted triangular tops and yellow trunks, over-sized faux-tree things with pink cottoncandy-esque tops, and the names of stores and their logos painted on the floor in enormous letters. Not pretty.

But I digress.

So I discover that being in a wheelchair does not accord me better treatment from people. No, they still just do their thing, get in the way, and in some ways are even worse. That causes me to be stopped from time to time, and it is then I discover one of the even stranger quirks of this mall: it vibrates. A lot. I feel it right through the wheels of the chair. Eerie!

Now as you know, I have that fixator attached to my leg. In order to keep it protected, there is one strut I can rest that leg on jutting forward from the base of the chair. Effectively, as mentioned before, it is like a bizarre lance, leading my way. Now beneath all that metal wrapped about my leg, like some odd medieval torture device, you can clearly see the nasty looking skin graft. At this point, it's still really pink, at some points a bit red and scabby, even, and just ugly. In deference to the human race, and to keep protected from the cold when traveling, I keep a flannel pillowcase about my fixator. It does hide, to a large degree, why I am bound to this damned wheelchair, admittedly.

Surmising that the human race needs to see why getting out of my way might be appreciated, I remove the pillowcase from the fixator-orbited leg. It's like Moses has parted the Red Sea. Seriously.

People get out of my way. In fact, I get somewhat of a wide berth. It reminds me of how an old friend in high school once cleared a path through dozens of people in a very crowded, shoulder-to-shoulder party. Loudly, he announced, "I think I'm gonna be sick!" and began to make retching noises. Clutching his mouth as though at any moment a vomitous mass might come thundering out, he aims in the direction he wants to go, and picks up speed. And the sea of humanity parts as though they had never been in his way. Same effect, less need for retching.

On the plus side, there are seats in the theater that are on main floor level, far enough back from the screen to allow a full view, and with normal seats so that those not bound to a chair with wheels can sit with their companion. Almost like how life was before I got smacked down by a car.

It was an almost normal day out. A nice change from my usual routine.

Thursday morning, six am. No consistency at all.

"Yes, good morning, Mr. Mushnik? This is Clarice, the visiting nurse. I will be arriving at your home in about an hour and a half."

Unlike sweet Allie and her delightful southern accent, Clarice is a middle aged woman who is no-nonsense, and a bit rough. That's it, I'm done. I called the right people, and got the number I needed.

"Yes, hi, this is Mr. Mushnik. I am done with your agency. No, not dying, nor checking back into the hospital. I can clean my own wound, thank you, and I have had it up to here with your lack of consistency. No, I am really going to be just fine without you. Thank you."

It was not hard to use the over-sized q-tip to swab my wound, and clean the area around the pins. In fact, doing it myself also meant I wasn't enduring having my temperature and blood pressure taken every single day, for no useful reason. Best of all, now I might be able to make more of the little sleep I am getting in the first place.

Chapter 12 – I am so gonna get medieval on your leg!

Thursday nights are the local SCA group meetings. Of course, it had been some eight weeks, or so, since I'd been able to attend. Tori planned to get me, and bring me out to this one. I was looking forward to yet another adventure outside my own four walls.

It should be mentioned that Tori's car was found, and returned to her. That's too bad, because it's a real piece of shit. Tori has also informed me that the clutch on my car is going. Well, shit. I mean, it's not like I don't have over one-hundred thousand miles on the thing. Still, something to get fixed. It's going to be tough to take the car in, when I still can't drive it.

Tori gets my chair down the stairs, and I head down on my ass, and soon we are loaded into the Jeep and en-route to the meeting. We meet in a small church in a town in northern New Jersey. The group has been meeting there for the entire three year period since I moved down here from college.

Now, several folks here besides Tori, Deb, Bob, and Sheila had paid visits to me during my hospitalization. Doug and his wife, Rachel, stopped in, Ivan had sent flowers, and several others had made a point of letting me know they were thinking about me. The SCA, as mentioned before, is like a second family, and these folks had become as close to me as a family. We'd do events together on weekends, and sometimes go on group outings to films and such, and we would spend other times together. We all do diverse things in the society, too, so it was pretty cool.

Visiting with everyone at the meeting was really good for my spirits. I don't think without all the care and support and good will I was constantly getting I could possibly have wanted to work so damned hard to recover.

My physical therapist loved that she could work me so hard. She really seemed to be pleased with my continued progress. I had even begun to work up enough strength to use the crutches for very short spans. I was still missing several muscle groups in my arm, and not much strength in most that were working, but it was something.

Did I mention that during all this, I went nearly two months without a proper bath or shower? No, I was not wretched and vile. I had gotten sponge baths in the hospital, and used a washcloth and such to clean myself. I could shower, but I had to sit on a special bench, and for a long time my leg had to be kept out of the water. After that visit to Dr. Weiss in the city, I was allowed to get my entire body wet. Of course, the water streaming from above while you are seated and unable to shift about can get really unpleasant. So I had a detachable shower-head, and used that to bathe. I was clean, but it was not nearly as satisfying as I remembered standing under the water for however long I chose could be.

I will take none of this lying down. I will stand. I will walk. I will heal.

Of course, it's about the time you are already down when you get bad news. Tori was visiting, I believe. I was in the living room, and my phone rang. I did not recognize the number, apart from a Chicagoland area code. So I picked it up.

"Hey Warren…it's Tobin."

"Toby! What's going on?"

I have not heard from Toby in years now. He was a part of my geeky High School choir room crowd, and graduated a couple years before I did. I knew he was living in the 'burbs somewhere, but we'd not spoken in years. I didn't even know he had my number.

"Look, Warren, I know it's been a while, but I have some sad news. Jeff passed away a couple days ago."

"What?"

Jeff and I had known one another since middle school. At one point, one after the other, we had even dated the same girl. We'd begun with somewhat of a rivalry, which evolved into a friendship. We sang the same voice part in choir, worked on the theater shows together. In fact, Jeff and I, along with Gary, who was my best friend in high school, were the bass trio. We sang together for over four years.

I had been home only, like, a year and a half prior for Jeff's wedding. I was just shy of six months older than Jeff.

"What happened?"

"He was working, and stood up at his desk. A co-worker apparently said, 'What's wrong?' and he'd replied 'I don't feel good,' and collapsed. They couldn't revive him. It was his heart."

"Holy shit."

"Yeah. Combined with a lot of stress and weight gain, they think he had a defect that went undetected from his youth. Nothing could be done for him."

"Wow. That sucks. So when's the funeral?"

"In a couple days. Can you come?"

Ah, so news had not gotten back home yet. "No, man. I'm kinda broken."

I relayed to Toby my own saga of woe. Not nearly so sad as Jeff's, but still not something the man needed to add to his thoughts.

"Shit, man. That sucks. You want me to relay your condolences to the family?"

"Please. Thanks, Toby. Tell everyone I am so sorry I cannot be there, but not to worry, I will recover."

"You got it, man. Take care."

I have never spoken to Toby since. We're friends on Facebook, but I don't believe, apart from wishing one-another a happy birthday, we've conversed. Gary, however, called a day or so later. That would be our first conversation in years, and the last since a brief e-mail years later, to which I responded, and never received more from.

Sometimes I look back at my lives--and yes, I do say lives. Back in the Midwest, before college was the first. Hell, before that, even when my parents were still together and we lived in Milwaukee. The third was college, and the years after, before my accident. The fourth is post-accident. Amazing the small and large things that can shape our lives in so many ways. Also amazing is this ability I have to constantly lose touch with the friendships from one life to the next. I wonder how many more times I will be reborn in this fashion?

Chapter 13 – Repairs continue.

After three months, Dr. Weiss determined it was time to do the bone graft to truly repair my leg.

Let's review, shall we?

To do the skin graft, they took what was essentially a fancy cheese slicer to remove a single layer of skin from my upper thigh, which they then grafted to the wound above my ankle.

And what about a bone graft?

That would be much more fun, I learned.

First, they would cut into the back of my hip. From that point, they would remove shavings of the bone. Those portions of bone would then be mixed in with a poultice of some sort that would then all be packed into the remains of my tibia.

Yes, it sounded pretty damned nasty to me, too.

There were, of course, some complicated aspects of the procedure. The first was the debate about having me completely out, under a general anesthetic, which they were not so thrilled with. I had already been completely under for at least one, if not both of my previous surgeries. So instead, they were planning to use a local, giving me a spinal and epidural anesthetic.

After this surgery, I can get the fixator removed, maybe sleep on my stomach again? Well, not necessarily, I'm told. It is possible that the graft might not take completely the first time, and they may have to do it again. And possibly a third time.

Oh no. No. Nope nope nope. That is bullshit. This will be done ONCE, and only once, and that will be ALL, thank you very much!

Yes, I had some pretty one-sided beliefs about the process. And I was only going to take so much. I was going to heal completely, and swiftly. I worked hard on that.

This seems as good a time as any to mention one of my "gifts". Now, admittedly, some people will think this bunk, and to you, all I can say is open your mind! I practice an art called Reiki. This is based on an ancient Japanese technique of hands on, and later, distance healing by manipulating energies. Moving energetic blocks out of and through the chakras, in order to heal the body. It was rediscovered by a Buddhist named Dr. Mikao Usui, in the early twentieth century, about 1922. While certainly not a replacement for traditional medicines, Reiki does no harm and is a good companion to normal techniques.

There are three primary levels in Reiki. The first is the ability to lay hands on a person, or one's self, to move and manipulate energy in order to open blockages and speed healing from pain and discomfort. To become a Reiki healer properly, one must seek out a Reiki master, who can pass them the attunements that will allow them to channel the energies and practice this healing art.

The second level allows for healing with the Reiki energy from a distance. Again, the master passes attunements, and you can then channel the energies at a distance to help someone in need.

The third level is the mastery. It used to cost as much as ten thousand dollars, and weeks of study with a Reiki master in order to be attained. Some masters, however, decided that that was denying a great number of energy workers their potential, and that the art is not something that should be hoarded and guarded like a prized secret, but shared and spread. More healers equals more healing and, at least in theory, the world becomes a better place.

Still, different Reiki masters take a different approach to the passing of attunements. Some masters take a weekend or two, or more, before passing each level on. Some prefer to allow for time between levels for the practitioner to get used to what they can do, and to practice and experience this skill with what they've got.

Now I don't mean to disparage the practice of passing on the attunements readily and easily so to speed the healing in the world at large, but there are some who pass it all in one weekend. Two days, and you go from no practice to being your own Reiki master. It strikes me as a bit extreme.

Another key point of Reiki is that it does not use your own energy. As a Reiki practitioner, you are a conduit. You pass on the energy that is in every aspect of the universe around you, as much or as little as the powers-that-be will send through you. There are other healing traditions similar to Reiki that involve using one's own energy, but that will degenerate this entire story into a lengthy discussion of energy healing, Wicca versus pagan traditions, and of course ESP and all inter-related sixth sense abilities.

Since we're here, this is as good a place as any to comment about my take on the six senses. Yes, I said six. We all know the basic five…taste, touch, sight, sound, and smell. But as much as many are totally unable to work the sixth, it is there none-the-less, and it falls into the general category of ESP.

Extra-sensory perception is not so illogical, if you consider a couple key points. The spectrum of light includes the visible, and then that which is beyond human visual acuity. We can't see ultraviolet or infrared. The senses work like this too, and we can't physically put a name to the sixth sense, but it is there anyhow, and I lump a lot of things into this sense. Much like modern string theory, however, and the whole idea that we can divide the universe into possibly as many as eleven dimensions, I am not about to suggest that we can divide our abilities into nine or ten senses. People have a hard enough time with the sixth. Among the extra-sensory talents, you will find clairvoyance, telepathy, telekinesis, energy healing, mediumship, and other similar sensibilities. While they are all different from one another, they all fall under the same philosophy.

There are a lot of frauds and phonies out there who will do bullshit readings or fake healings, or commune with the dead to persuade you to donate all your cash to the Church of Foamy, but the reason the frauds can even exist is because of those who truly are in touch with those abilities.

My own talents in the sixth sense realm are not something I discuss readily with people. A lot of folks are just not ready to accept, and cannot understand my gifts. Now this is not meant to be bragging, I am just telling it like it is. I have been told that I am an excellent Reiki healer, and that my empathy and my ability to read people are rather impressive.

Yes, I said read people.

"What does that mean," you ask?

In general, but not always, I can see into the depths of a person's personality in a matter of minutes after meeting them. I can get a sense of the kind of person they are, what they believe with regards to treating other people, and how they want to be treated and respected. I am obviously not always accurate, but ninety percent of the time I am spot on. I don't mention it much because it can put people off. Even people with energetic shields and barriers in place seldom can keep me from reading them.

All this gets into a far more complicated aspect of these abilities, and bears a little need for explanation. If you've been reading this without a bathroom break, now might be a good place to pause before moving on.

Chapter 14 – …but I digress.

Step into my mind, and see how I view the universe around me.

This might be a wild ride. Make sure you didn't just eat. No vomiting allowed!

Here is what I believe: We, and everything else you can see and not see, are made of energy. At our core, like every star, drop of water, electron or whole galaxy we are made of energy. Science!

As such, there are energies everywhere. They flow, they ebb, they are like a river that is always in motion. Yoda and the Jedi didn't really have it wrong. "Luminous beings are we, not this crude matter," as Yoda said. The energy is created by life. It surrounds us, penetrates us, and binds the galaxy together - much like duct tape. Unlike the Force, the energy that I comprehend the universe to hold is neither light nor dark; it is grey. Again, like duct tape. It is only colored by the intent of one wielding that energy, or directing its flow, if you will. Apart from that, it remains neutral.

Anyhow, a lot of people besides me comprehend this energy, but not in the same manner that I do. They don't necessarily see it as neutral; they see it as black or white, good or bad, etc. As such, a lot of people put up blocks, shields, barriers, or what-have-you, so they feel they are protecting themselves. I have found that such blocks really offer no protection, and in fact, can have the opposite effect. The energies flow. And if you block the flow, like any dam that does not occasionally relieve the pressure, you will have a flood. Floods of energy can be bad. Not bad as in the opposite of good, bad as in too much for us to handle all at once.

Keeping that in mind, the key I have discovered is to accept that the energy needs to flow, so you need to let it flow through you. The mistake a lot of those people make, and mind you this is simply my not-so-humble opinion, is that, if they sense and feel this energy, they need to caress it, to feel it, to touch it. Even if they don't choose to use it in some way, they still connect to it, and that is the problem.

Rather than shield, rather than block, it is better to let it flow through, but not to touch it. Easier said than done. The energies can be very very powerful. So, a lot of people who can channel and feel and connect to this energy will, given the chance, take it into themselves.

That's not always a bad thing, mind you, but it can cause a lot of problems. The blocks people put up, rather than allowing the flow, can cause a back-up, and even a back-flow, that can do harm, usually to them. You get what you give when it comes to energy.

I have shown more than one person that allowing the flow to pass through and around you is not a bad idea.

Like I said, Mr. Mushnik's wild ride.

Please don't lock me away. I am not crazy. Just differently sane.

Note to self – the sequel! Write a lengthier discussion of the many and varying abilities that make up what we call the sixth sense, from ESP, to energy healing, to clairvoyance, to telekinesis. Yeah, I have my own theories about all this, and it might be interesting, now that I have put this to text, to explain that we may have more than six senses, but we'll just save that for another story. Or maybe, in the future, I'll become a blogger. There's an idea.

Still digressing, but back to one of my original points. An acquaintance of mine from the SCA had been through a one-weekend Reiki course, and gone from zero to Reiki master in two days. She was one of my visitors while I was convalescing at Helen Hayes. She decided to practice some Reiki on me while I was resting in my bed one afternoon.

I love Reiki. Giving it, receiving it, it really doesn't matter. But she made an error that irritated me. She did not just act as a pure conduit for the energy, she took it into herself first, colored it with her own ego, and then passed it on. This felt - wrong.

I did not know what else to do. Her energy was beginning to almost burn, and I only meant to put up a block of sorts, to cease the flow. But later she would relay to me that I switched her off.

Ok, now we get into an entire idea that could once more take up the whole of this story. I know that some of you reading this are already shaking your head, and going,"Geez, what a freak! This started out about severe injuries, and now we're discussing the Hooky-spooky freakazoid energy bullcrap thing. Get on with it!"

You see, my reader, this energy bullcrap is a part of who I am. I have connections with these things that go beyond my Reiki abilities, and that defy a simple explanation. So let's just say I have a lot of knowledge and abilities on varied and diverse levels.

At any rate, when I reached out to block her energy, it seems I overdid it a little. I was later told she could channel nothing at all for a good week after that.

Oops.

Despite the long digression, back to my original point. I had been practicing Reiki on myself often, to speed along my healing. I had already regained more use of my arm than they'd expected in four and a half months, and I would be damned if I would take the full year to three years to walk again. Ergo - one bone graft. That would be all.

Chapter 15 – ORs and Recovery rooms and Wards, oh my!

The morning of the surgery came damned early. Good grief, why did I need to be at pre-op at oh-god-it's-six-am? We sat and waited, my dad and stepmom, and me. Surgery number three. I was getting really tired of going under the knife.

Before this accident, I had only broken two bones in my life, and only had surgery to close a couple scars. In third grade, I broke the pinky finger of my right hand playing kickball. In middle school, I wiped out skiing and fractured my knee, though I did not learn that I had fractured it until years later, when I badly sprained that same knee. My pain tolerance is high. I skied and walked on a fractured knee, and did not know it was that badly injured until seven years later.

Anyhow, we wait - and wait. And at long last, they come for me.

I hate this.

The OR is cold. That, I remember. And I was on my stomach, since they were taking the bone from the back of my hip and grafting it into my leg from the back. I felt the needle, and damn, do I hate needles! Then the sedative took effect - and I faded out. While they only gave me a local anesthetic, they gave me enough to essentially knock me out, so I have no memory of the procedure.

When I came back around, it was cold. Really cold. Brrrrrrrrrr, someone turn-up-the-damned-heat-before-my-teeth-start-to-chatter cold. I learned the OR was kept awful close to freezing – germs don't do so well at that temp, but damn, I wasn't so well, either!

For some reason, I was still in the OR, even though they were done with me. I learned later that they were a bit over-crowded in recovery.

I was now on my back, and still totally numb from the waist down. I had no idea just what they'd done to me, but didn't expect it was going to be too pleasant.

They finally wheel me into the recovery room, and they cover me with warm blankets. That is good, as I am indeed shivering from the cold now.

Recovery is a strange place. Lots of equipment beeping and chirping, and so on and so forth, doctors and nurses talking, and grunts and groans mixed with other sounds of pain and discomfort from the patients. On top of all that, I had a blood pressure machine attached to my arm, constantly getting tighter as it checked, then loosening, then repeating it again. The room was lit by fluorescent lights, and I had one that was more or less in my eyes the whole time. The blood pressure thing was very aggravating. Squeeze, pressure -release. About every ten minutes or so.

And the light was really annoying.

I was uncomfortable, just in general - and thirsty. Really, really thirsty. It had been, by now, something like 15 hours, or more, since the last food or drink I'd had.

It took forever to get a nurse to finally let me have some water, and damn was that a sweet and refreshing drink!

To make it just that much more uncomfortable, the guy next to me was intubated, and awake, and clearly even more uncomfortable than me. I could only hear him; we were all partitioned off from one another, in recovery.

It seemed that, for some reason, they did not have a room prepared for me yet. That was why I was still in recovery.

As if all that was not enough fun…the epidural was wearing off. I am not sure what was hurting more at this point, the back of my leg, or my hip. But I knew I was not a happy camper, and I was beginning to want a pain killer, as well as a room with no light so I could sleep it off.

It seemed like I was in recovery forever. It might have been only an hour, it may have been several, but between the increasing soreness and the noise and light, I really wanted out.

It all happened at once, of course. They were starting to move me out, finally, when they stopped in order to inject morphine into the IV.

I expect I will remember that moment with clarity like it only just happened, for the rest of my life. I learned that morphine doesn't actually dull the pain. No, it makes you stop caring that you are in pain. Seriously.

Damn, I hurt, but - I just don't care.

This was my only thought, after the morphine took hold.

However, the moment after the narcotic was added to my IV, every nerve ending in my body lit up as if I were a match that had just been struck. I gasped, I tensed, and then it was gone and I stopped caring that I was in pain.

They took me to a room, moved me to a bed, and I was out. In the morning, I was feeling less sore, but realized that, crap, I had been catheterized again. Damn, is that an unpleasant sensation.

Sometime that morning, the nurse came in, and I learned that I was in the wrong ward. They did not seem to have enough room in the orthopedic ward, so I was in the brain injury ward with stroke patients and such. That meant the doctor would be slow in getting to me, which I did not relish. I was beginning to thoroughly dislike hospitals at this point. Eventually, that dislike turned into a full phobia, complete with panic attacks, but that's another story, too.

Without ceremony, nor warning, the nurse removes my catheter. I would not be surprised if my scream is still echoing around that ward, years later. Yup, that really fucking hurt. My penis is not meant to have a tube inserted, then removed from it, thank you very much. Strictly exit only. And there is nothing quite as uncomfortable as a catheter.

Oversharing? Maybe…but that's the point of this entire story, so suck up and deal with it.

In time, my doctor paid me a visit. I learned that, though I could not see them, there were now staples up the back of my leg, and also along the back of my hip. Once I was released, though, I could bathe. That was a good thing. The surgery went well. In time, we'd see how much the graft took, or if it needed to be done again.

Like I said, one shot. That was going to be all.

Of course I received visitors on and off again. Some of the usual folks, and even one or two surprises. It was nice to feel so loved. It was good to see that so many people cared. After only two days, they let me go home. Sooner than the hospital administrator would have normally liked, but given how quickly I returned to as normal as I could achieve at this point, the doctor thought it best I get to be home. So dad and Lucy came, and soon I was back in my apartment with my cat.

Chapter 16 – I swear the walls are closing in!

There were, of course, times when the walls of my apartment seemed to be closing in around me. Being unable to come and go as I please was often frustrating, and wheeling about the apartment in the chair was not terribly satisfying. I may be a fat, overweight man, but that does not mean I am inactive. But that was not always healthy.

I did writing, as best I could with a barely-working right hand. At first I did a lot of lefty typing, which was slow, but doable. In time I began to recover more use of my right, which made things quite a bit easier. I composed a poem or two along the way, or rather, that which I attempt to pass off as poetry. It's more of a rambling prose most of the time.

It just so happened that around this time poor Bob lost his job. This did, however, present an up-side. I would be sitting around, bored with the TV, when there would be a random knock at my door - and there was Bob.

"C'mon, buddy. I bet you need to get out of here!"

Amen, brother.

So Bob would serve a dual purpose. One, he got me the hell out of my apartment, and two, he got my car back on the road.

You just cannot leave a car un-driven for too long. I mean, things seize up, and the poor thing doesn't like to start, and blah blah blah. So Bob, being capable of driving a car with manual transmission, would take mine out with me.

We didn't do anything terribly interesting. We drove around Rockland County, we'd sometimes venture into New Jersey. We'd grab lunch. We'd chat about people, and things, and so on. Nothing very exciting, but it certainly beat just sitting around my house, wanting to poke my eyes out.

A week after the third surgery, I went to Doctor Weiss' Rockland office. There were, in order to close the wounds this new surgery had made, staples in the back of my leg, as well as my hip. Yup, metal staples, and they, of course, need to come out - one at a time.

No, I kid you not. One staple at a time. He removed them with something like a pliers. Pluck. Pluck. Pluck. It was not pleasant - not in the least. Now mind you, this is on top of numerous other unpleasantries. I mean, c'mon, I have this satellite system orbiting my right leg, plates embedded in my right shoulder, and almost constant pain.

It's really amazing how your perspective is altered when it's not a question of "are you in pain?" but rather, "how much pain are you currently experiencing?"

To all the masochists out there, pardon my saying so, but – you're fucking insane. Pain is *not* a good thing. Just sayin.

Chapter 17 – I'm not fencing, but I can still keep the rest of you playing safe!

Sometime after that latest experience, Bob took me along to an SCA event in the group about an hour south of me. It was a big, annual event, where normally I would be fencing. Obviously, I was still not able to fence, and mostly wheelchair bound.

It was a chilly March afternoon. I was dressed in one of my tunics, and my usual obnoxious pants with the buttons along the side, so that I could put them on even with the fixator on my leg. On top of that, I had a flannel pillowcase covering the fixator.

It's time for another overshare. Ok, so I had no choice but to wear pants that opened along the side to allow me to get them over/around the damned fixator. That presented another inconvenience: I could not wear underwear. Now, some of you, I am sure, have no problem going "regimental", but I do. It's the stupid little things that can be the most annoying.

I get to the event, and even though it is chilly, it's not too chilly for my fellow fencers to be outside. I got myself wheeled down the hill to where the fencers were gathered. Many were surprised to see me. I saw quite a few folks I had only briefly seen, if at all, since my injury.

Porsche was there, along with her boyfriend, Peter. Porsche and I had been fencing together since I moved here, and even though we did not get along in the beginning, we have since become good friends.

Digression: This is a recurrent pattern in my life. People will start off disliking me, and then, somewhere along the way, things change, and they start to like me and become an ally. Weird. Of course, conversely, people who start off as friends and confidants sometimes do a complete one-eighty, and become opponents, and such. I seem to always have it one or the other, seldom finding folks in the middle. What is it about my personality that is so polarizing? Something to ponder.

There were a number of folks like Johan and Zachary and Maren and others who I'd fenced with at practice and events over the years. It was really good to see them all.

Jon, who at this time was the head of all fencing in the Kingdom, was also there. He came to me, and started joking.

"So, uh, William - you know that thing's not list legal?" He was referring to the fixator.

"Yeah, well, I thought I'd try to get it passed as a new rigid parry item." That made them laugh.

"Here to watch?" someone asked.

"No, I figure I can marshal, at least."

I had a job to do!

In modern fencing, it's about coaches and judges. In the SCA, we have marshals. A marshal is kind of an odd combo of coach and judge, like a traffic cop, to keep the participants and spectators equally safe. From my wheelchair, I marshaled some bouts.

"Ok, are you both satisfied with each other's arms, armor, and blah blah blah? Good, make salutes to the crowd, crown, inspiration, and your noble and worthy opponent." Salutes happened, and they were ready. "Take your guards. Honor before glory, lay on!"

And thus combat would begin.

SCA fencing is very different from what you see in the Olympics, or at colleges. We are in much more colorful outfits, not whites, for one. In fact, our rules push a person to get out of the standard whites, or at least cover them with something that looks period. Next, we don't fight on a strip, we fight in the round. We will circle, we will shift about. Heck, give us obstacles and we'll fight over/around and even through them.

Then there are the weapons. Most of us have been moving away from the standard foils and epees into the heavier, more realistic schlagers. These blades are either an oval or diamond cross section, and they have a definite flat and edge distinction. They also weigh more than the other weapons, vary in length, and can have a more ornate guard, with openings and twisted metal and such. Only a matter of time until we retire foils and epees completely, I suspect.

In addition to that, we sometimes fight with more than one weapon. That can take multiple forms, such as a sword in each hand, a sword and dagger, or a shield/buckler or cloak. Even without a secondary weapon, we use the hand to block shots, figuring losing a hand beats "getting killed," as it were. Thus, using both hands is a regular occurrence. It makes for a very interesting, spirited game.

Anyhow, the fights that afternoon were the usual, with one exception. Johan and Jon went at it, and they went waaaaaaaaaaaaay out, and I was marshaling. It was a good five minutes before another noticed me.

"Are you watching that bout out there?"

"Yup."

"They been at it a while now?"

"Yup. Neither wants to commit to anything."

"Damn."

Eventually, someone twitched, and I believe Johan lost to Jon. Jon has been the King's rapier champion numerous times, so it was no shock.

It should probably be mentioned that, in addition to the marshals versus non-marshals, there is a sort of hierarchy among the fencers in the SCA. In the East, there are two forms this takes. One is the peer (small 'p' as in contemporary) recognized/promoted system, called the League of Rapier Academies. Maren actually refers to this as the "faux super-hero league," and would later dub me Titanium Lad. But in this setting, we have four ranks, recognized and advanced purely from within. The other, in most respects bigger award, is given by the crown. This is called the Order of the Golden Rapier, which is abbreviated as OGR. That award is given for a combination of skill, service, and a certain je ne sai que that defies explanation. With the award, the recipients usually take the title of Don or Doña, gender specific.

Jon and Johan are Dons, Maren and Porsche are Doñas. Damn, do I want to be a Don someday. Fencing is the only sport I have ever had even a vague skill in, and I want that acknowledged by my peers. Very much. Probably too much. That will take a while. I can't currently stand, let alone fence.

Another thing I do in the SCA is archery. Yeah, that is going to be tough, too. Rather hard to pull a bow, when your arm is next to useless. It gets really really frustrating sometimes. Now you have gotten a glimpse into what passes as my social life. It makes me happy, and is a lot of fun and cool people.

Chapter 18 – Would the real Warren Mushnik please stand up?

About this time, I had developed enough strength in my right arm, or more specifically my shoulder and triceps and lats, to begin to use crutches. It was not easy, at first, but I began to get more and more proficient. My in-home physical therapist was pleased to help me work them more and more. She would help me do things to strengthen those arm muscles, so I might be able to use the crutches more frequently. It was still difficult, of course. My right leg could not touch the ground and bear any weight at that time, and the fixator meant I had to be careful not to catch it on the crutch. Still, I found some way to maneuver with it, and get around.

I went to visit Doctor Weiss in early April, following my latest x-ray, and entered his office on crutches. I had left the wheelchair at home.

"Damn. Didn't expect that," he stated. Clearly, again, I was defying the prognosis.

He examined the x-ray, looking at the bone graft specifically.

"Well, it does seem to be taking," he remarked. "We might be able to remove the fixator in three weeks or so, and put you in a walking cast."

"Really?"

I could hardly believe this.

"It's possible. Also…you can start to bear about twenty-percent weight on the leg. Get a scale, and measure out pressure to twenty pounds. No more than that, but try to do a little every day."

"Okay."

I could hardly believe the fixator might be coming off soon. I was beyond tired (pun unintended) of being forced to sleep on my back. The idea of sleeping on my belly again was too good to not get excited about.

It is not secret I have never been so good at sleep. I don't seem to ever get enough of it. It does not matter when I go to bed, or how late I attempt to sleep in, I rarely get more than seven hours. Sometimes a shade more, but usually closer to four to six. Being forced to sleep on my back only made matters worse.

I acquired a scale, and put my foot down - literally. Let me tell you, those pins in the bottom of my foot are not comfortable.

You learn a lot about yourself in six months, when you are spending most of your time with yourself. Yeah, sure, Bob comes by a couple times a week and kidnaps me to get me the hell out of here, and Tori comes by often, and Dad and Lucy, and Jill. Other friends pop by from time to time, but for the most part, I spend a lot of time alone. I can't work, and even though I have acquired a speech recognition program for the computer, it's pretty damned clunky. I think the technology to really get this thing working is a few more years off. Close, but not completely accurate, yet. But I am writing, and I have slowly regained more use of my right hand and arm.

I am twenty seven years old…and very fortunate that I have made it more than half way into my twenty seventh year. How close did I come to death? That's a question I don't know that I want answered. Will I remember what actually happened to me, down the line? Again, another question to which I might not necessarily want the answer.

Do I love Tori? I mean, she has been here for me all throughout this ordeal; she's really made a point of showing me how much she cares. But somehow, I have not managed to remain faithful to her. We are not, technically, a couple, but we still spend a lot of time together like a couple, and we are still having sex. Hooray for my genitals remaining undamaged.

Then there is Jill. So young, so fragile, and so in love with me. How do I feel about Jillian? She pops by to visit, from time to time as well, and most times we wind up having sex. I'm not in love with her, either. At least, I really don't think. So what am I doing?

Do I love either of these women in my life? Or both? Or neither? Is it just lust? Certainly the pleasure of sexual contact beats out the daily pain of my injuries, but what am I doing? How badly am I hurting either of them - or both of them?

So what does this make me? What kind of man am I? Yes, I know, I am an asshole for using both women this way. I will only defend myself by saying that neither of them is without getting something out of our connections as well, but I am still the villain in this piece, make no doubt about that.

Before my accident, I had just left a temp job. Since college, I have bounced from job to job, never settling for more than a couple of years at a time into any one thing. I am either quickly bored by what I am doing, or otherwise put off my game. Like my relationships, my jobs never fully satisfy me. Damn am I indecisive. I think. Or maybe not. I don't know, am I indecisive?

Anyhow, I was between jobs, once again, when some bastard used a car to bowl me down. So, the next question is: in a karmic sense, did I bring this on to myself? Sure, in theory, it's possible. Maybe in the next life for some of my actions, I might be chancing coming back to this world as a slug, and being salted, but maybe in this life, I am getting my comeuppance here and now. And maybe I am seriously overthinking this whole situation.

Do I believe what Tori says, that Consciousness Creates Reality? I don't know...maybe. I believe that I will heal completely, and that is the only reality I envision for my future. Is that what she is talking about?

I have never been a religious man. Hell, before I got involved with Tori, I'm not sure I would even have called myself a spiritual man, but I believe that I can heal from this misadventure. I can completely recover from these wounds. But the big question is – do I return to where I was, or push forward to be more, to be greater?

Chapter 19 – Re-casting this whole piece.

So, the next three weeks roll along, and I return to Dr. Weiss' office. I am nervous with anticipation. Do I get to move on? Does this damned fixator come off my leg? How much longer will I be in this position? The wheelchair has been left at home. In fact, most of my time traveling now is without the wheelchair. I have become strong enough, and agile enough, to maneuver most everywhere on my crutches.

It seems like an eternity before Dr. Weiss sees me. I have already been to another office to be x-rayed, and I have brought the films along with me. Once he gets to me, the doctor looks the x-rays over, and I am so completely impatient it's got to be tangible to both him, and my father. He nods his head.

"Okay, we can remove the fixator."

I think I might well have teared up on that statement. Little did I know what I was in for now, though. We went into a different examination room, this one with a standard table. There would be no need for me to remove any clothing or such, and my dad could remain here. Dr. Weiss was just going to take off the fixator. He has a bunch of tools that make it look like he's really going to repair a car. There is something simply not right about being with a doctor who is using a pair of pliers and other similar tools to work on you.

He begins by removing the various external bits. Plates and other metal parts that have made up the satellite system orbiting my lower leg. It is not a comfortable process; there are a lot of pieces that have gone into this miraculous device that, externally, held my leg bones together.

Oh, a brief note: the bone graft, which, pleasantly, took the first time around, has made my tibia and fibula become permanently fused together. That means, I have been told, that chances are I will walk with a limp for the rest of my life.

We'll see.

So, at last there are just the pins. There are nine of them, sticking out of various bones and through the skin of my leg. I can't imagine his removing those is going to feel very pleasant. He begins by working on the left side pin in my foot. Thus far, he hasn't done anything to address any prospective pain or discomfort. As he torques the pin, I feel the skin holding to it break - on both sides of my foot.

Oh fuck. That isn't a pair of pins sticking out of my foot. It's one pin, and it passes all the way through. You're kidding, right? Is there going to be anesthetic of some sort applied at any time during this procedure? Anybody? Anybody?

Then the first pin, the one that I thought was two at the bottom of my foot, is yanked out.

Yanked out. Pulled. Ripped from the skin and muscle and bone it was screwed into.

Ouch.

Yup. This hurt a lot.

Then, he began with one of the ones in my ankle. There are four there, right? Oh no. There are two. These, too, pass all the way through my leg. This is not gonna be fun.

Please tell me there is some sort of topical anesthetic that will be applied, right? You're going to do something to ease the pain, right? Oh no, Dr. Weiss twists the pin. Fuck that hurts. He gives it a slight tug, and it begins to come out. He pulls again, and soon the pin is clear of my ankle. I don't know how loud my cries were. But damn did that hurt.

Now, he begins on the next pin in my ankle. I no longer question if there are in fact two. It's obviously just one pin passing all the way through my ankle.

"Is…is there any way you can do something for the pain? Isn't there some way you can make this hurt less?"

"Sorry, Warren. It's this, or you go to the emergency room to have this done."

Sigh. "Okay."

He yanks the pin, and it gets about halfway out. He tugs, and tugs. It's caught on something. Fuck does that hurt.

Sigh.

"You'll probably need to push it back through, and pull it back out the other side, then."

"Yup."

And he did. No warning, no advance notice of any sort. Suddenly Dr. Weiss just shoves this pin that was halfway out of my leg back the way it came. I think he caught a nerve cluster on the way out.

I know I screamed. God damn did that hurt!

Okay, to all you ladies reading this who say a man cannot understand the pain of giving birth, I would bet you that I can. I mean, c'mon, sure there is that whole pushing a watermelon through an opening meant for a lime, but I have had a metal pin shoved through muscle and skin where it was never meant to be. I can relate. Even if I can't, let me just sympathetically say, *"Ouch!"*

I think it was about this time Dr. Weiss turned to my father.

"Mr. Mushnik? You might want to close the door; he might be scaring the other patients."

Oh, you think? And I joked that the fixator was some sort of medieval torture device. How right was I?

There were two pins remaining. These two were thicker, and had been attached below the knee to the unbroken bone. Thankfully, once he untorqued them, their removal was not nearly so painful as the rest had been. Just like that, the fixator was in pieces, and attached to my leg no more, but damn were those wounds unattractive! Dr. Weiss salved some kind of reddish purple goo onto my wounds, but did not dress them. He began soon after to apply the bandaging that would be my cast.

I had not yet let go of the edges of the examination table. I wouldn't be the least surprised if, to this day, that table still has my fingerprints embedded in its underside.

Did I mention fucking ow?

Anyhow, it was not long before Dr. Weiss had a cast around my leg, and it was a cast that could bear weight.

"So this is a full walking cast?" I questioned.

"Yes."

"How soon can it bear full weight?"

"As soon as you want to try it."

"What about driving?"

He shrugged.

"The cast is on your right leg and right foot. If you can figure out some way to work the pedals, you can drive. Your ankle is not going to move."

"You think your arm is strong enough for you to steer and shift, Warren?" my dad asked, seriously.

I didn't have the answers.

"Do you want to take home the pins? We can't reuse those," Dr. Weiss informs me.

"Uh, sure."

Souvenirs of my leg-orbiting satellite. Maybe someday I will turn them into a work of art somehow.

"You are free to go. Take care."

So I hopped off the table, onto my left leg. My right leg seemed so much smaller, and lighter. I put my foot down. Even using the crutches, I bore as much weight as I could stand.

That night, I rolled onto my stomach to sleep. It was still not quite right, but I could lie there without my poor foot floating in space above the covers. I think I cried myself to the best night's sleep I had had in seven months.

Chapter 20 – Maybe you should drive.

A couple of days after the fixator removal, Tori came to visit. We took my car out to an empty parking lot not far from home, and we changed places. It was not easy to work the pedals with a cast on my leg, and my arm had to, more or less, rest on the gear shift, but I found that if I toed the pedals, I could accelerate, and break. I even practiced slamming on the breaks, and found that, to my surprise, I could drive. That meant I would be done with my in-home therapists, and I would soon begin outpatient therapy, back at Helen Hayes.

One reason I had wanted to be able to drive was to go to a wedding in Massachusetts. My old college roommate, Anne, was getting married. There was still some concern that I would not be safe driving all the way up to Cape Cod on my own, and Tori was not available. Certainly, I could not take Jillian, as we were publicly pretending to not be speaking. The solution? My sister decided to come for a visit, and join me at the wedding. I packed up my gear, and soon Marnie and I were loaded into the car.

My sister Marnie is five years my junior. She and I have always gotten along well, even though she can be a know-it-all brat. It's kind of funny, but she had spent time with Anne and the gang when we were all in college, so it seemed somewhat appropriate that she should be coming with me to this wedding. Marnie had graduated from college last year, and was still living in one of the Chicago suburbs, making some use of her degree. We look nothing alike, my sister and I. She is thin, and far lighter haired than I. But there are certainly moments when it is completely clear that she is, without a doubt, my sister.

Together, we took my first trek away from home, not to a hospital or doctor's appointment, or the mall, or an SCA meeting, or just out to get me clear of my apartment, in over seven months. There was something very freeing about this trip.

Daily I put more weight on my foot. It hurt a lot, but I decided that if I did not bear as much weight as I could, it would take longer to heal. I drove for a long way, before Marnie complained that she had come along in part to do some of the driving. So we stopped, grabbed a bite to eat, and Marnie took the wheel.

My dear sister claimed she was fully capable of driving a stick shift. If that was the case, then why was she having so much trouble with first gear? It was not a problem for much of the drive, until we hit some nasty traffic, snarling up a hill, en route to Cape Cod.

It was somewhere in all of this that I flashed back to when Marnie was learning to drive.

I was twenty, and home from college for some reason or other. Marnie was fifteen, and had a learner's permit. So of course, she wanted her big brother to take her out driving. She figured that, maybe, it would be more constructive than the similar trips with mom. We fight occasionally, my sister and I, but it is nothing like the way she and mom go at it. We were at the lot of a local mall, and Marnie got behind the wheel. I am pretty certain at that point, I was still driving my first car, a lovely 1984 Subaru. It was a solid car, if not the prettiest on the road.

So we start along, and at the first traffic light Marnie hits the breaks hard, causing us both to jolt forward.

"Easy, sis, anticipate that you are going to have to stop."

"What does that mean?" she snips.

"It means, when the light turns yellow, take your foot off the gas, and coast for as long as you can. Then, you won't need to apply the break so hard."

A reasonable explanation, no?

The light turns green, and we roll along again, up to the next light turning yellow, then red. Marnie jolts us forward when she breaks, once again.

"What did I tell you about anticipating the stop?"

"Don't snap at me!" she insists.

I didn't snap; I reiterated my point.

"Just relax. Driving tense does no one any good."

"Don't tell me how to drive," she snaps.

"If I am not supposed to tell you how to drive, then what is the point of this lesson, kiddo?"

She had no answer for that. It went a bit better, until we were moving along a fairly dull two lane local road, and she switched lanes without even a glance in her mirror, or out a window. We nearly side-swiped a car in that move.

"Hey, kid, be careful! You can't change lanes without looking!"

"I signaled!" she responded, instantly defensive.

"That's good, but you didn't look," I point out.

"Stop telling me how I'm doing this wrong! You're sounding just like mom."

"Fine. Pull over."

She got all silent and indignant, but pulled over. We traded places. That was the end of the lesson, for what it was worth. That was also the last time I attempted to tell Marnie how to drive. Incidentally, that remains a sore spot years later. I am pretty certain, to this day, Marnie will maintain that she is an excellent driver, and I am a lousy driver. She will also point out that she scored higher than I did when she took her driver's test. Gotta love siblings.

Back on our road trip to Cape Cod, Marnie actually only argued with me briefly, when we were on that hill, and I insisted that she let me do the driving again. She may have fought me more, had she not just stalled out for the third time.

Eventually, we made it to the wedding.

It was good to see everyone again. I don't know when the last time was that Anne, Sarah, Ed and I were together. Of course, Sarah's sister Anne was with us, as was her husband, Tom. And the gang would have been incomplete without Carla being there, too.

College, far from home, had been quite the adventure. I met Sarah and Ed first. Through Sarah I met Anne, her roommate. The four of us, along with a few others from time to time, would become quite the group throughout our years in Ithaca. Ed and Anne dated for a time. It ended, and they remained friends. Anne and Sarah, though very very different personalities, would be roommates, beginning the second semester of freshman year, and lasting all throughout college. By junior year, Ed and I roomed together. Then the four of us, and a fifth, got an apartment off campus for senior year. Thus began the debacle of the fifth housemate.

The four of us were platonic friends, and apart from Ed and Anne's relationship, that was all we ever were. Ed, junior year, was seeing an interesting girl, who was in the theater program with me. We had decided, as a group, to acquire a five bedroom apartment, really close-to but off-campus. Ed and his girlfriend would technically live in the large, master bedroom, even though the fifth room would be "hers" to show the parents should they visit. We each had our own decent-sized room, and shared the living room, kitchen, etc. We even had two bathrooms, one on each floor.

"You'll be alright if you two break up, right?" someone queried.

"Oh, yes," Ed's girlfriend said.

I can't recall who the clairvoyant was. Shock and dismay, Ed and his girl break up. Shock two, she can't live with us. Right. But we need to have a fifth housemate, still.

Enter Suzi and her cat, Katze. Katze is an ancient calico, but a totally sweet cat. And Suzi has graduated, but plans to live in Ithaca for the year, partying with friends, just generally putting together a life. Suzi is a fraternity sister of Sarah's. Go figure, co-ed service frat. Anyhow, we are not, technically, supposed to have a cat. But since Katze is ancient, she's certainly going to be flying under the radar most of the time.

This part is largely hearsay, but from what I gathered, somewhere along in her senior year, Suzi had seduced one of her professors. He was not much to look at, nor much respected, but she had a thing for him anyhow. It becomes doubly interesting when you take into account that Suzi claimed to be a lesbian throughout most of college. So there we were, end of our junior year, with Suzi graduated, and we moved into our apartment in the spring. Suzi goes downtown to the bars one night, and runs into Mr. Professor. They have drinks together; she goes home with him. They have sex. Unprotected sex.

A few weeks later...she informs us she is pregnant with Mr. Professor's child. We so should have been on *The Real World.*

Suzi originally planned to remain with us, and we, initially, went with that idea. On further examination, however, I concluded that having a pregnant woman, and then a baby, in our apartment during our senior year of college was simply not a great idea. It turned out, Ed concurred. To my surprise, so did Sarah. We didn't need to ask Suzi to leave, however. She opted to take Katze and return to her parents' home to have her baby. She wanted a girl, which I don't doubt she'd have tried to persuade to be a lesbian. The universe, with its infinite sense of humor, gave her a boy.

With Katze's departure, Anne and I, in particular, found we missed having a cat. Neither Ed nor Sarah were adverse to the idea, so we went to the local SPCA, and adopted one. That is how I came into the possession of my dear cat, Shira. I named her, and then paid to have her fixed, so she became mine. My dear sweet calico kitty, who is somewhere around here even as I compose this.

It would be several months before we acquired a fifth housemate. We had no choice; we could not leave the room vacant or the rent unpaid, and we could not afford to split the fifth rent between the four of us. I don't believe the management of the complex would allow that anyhow. Enter Nate. Nate was a junior, and familiar to myself and Sarah in particular. He was a good guy. Well, one day, Nate caught a message being left on his answering machine for his roommate. Said message was telling him about a forthcoming drug delivery. Nate, cop-wannabe, turned the tape in to the campus police. His roommates' dealer was busted with six hundred tabs of acid. His roommate was then busted with one hundred and fifty. Nate was a bit nervous about how he would be treated if they found him, since they knew it was due to him they'd been caught.

We had a spare room. Nate's roommate did not know us. Nate moved in. Thus the saga of the fifth housemate debacle more or less closed. The rest is both dry and totally unnecessary to the overall story I am relaying here.

Anyhow, Anne's wedding was to Barry. Barry was the second man to whom Anne had been engaged. After senior year, she had actually been engaged to a man named Daniel. Daniel and Anne had a long, twisted relationship, filled with cheating and ugly fights and other strange occurrences. It was actually out of the blue that Anne ended that relationship, just a couple weeks before the wedding. In fact, the weekend of her planned co-ed bachelorette party. We still had that party. We took a limo all over Ithaca and Cortland, and had a grand old time. But she and Daniel were through.

Barry was a much better match. We celebrated their nuptials, and had an excellent reunion. After the wedding, Marnie and I returned home. I put Marnie on a plane back to Chicago, and returned to what there was of my life.

Chapter 21 – Checking in for Outpatient therapy.

It was at this point that I began my outpatient therapy at Helen Hayes. With the walking cast, and my ability to drive, we did a twice-a-week session. First occupational therapy, working on recovering my arm, and then physical therapy, to increase my mobility.

On my first trek to Helen Hayes, I crutched my way over to the ward I had spent three weeks in, and visited the nurses' station. The nurses were very happy to see me upright and on crutches. Before I could say anything, they asked how I was doing.

"I am much better, thank you. It's good to see you again."

They were a little stunned at that. Took me a moment to realize why. After the doctors at the hospital had scratched my vocal cords, it would not be until after I'd gotten home, as mentioned previously, that I recovered my voice. The nurses remembered me with a high, raspy, scratchy, whisper of a voice. Now I stood before them with my normal voice, seemingly, emanating from somewhere around my toes. I have often said, while I may only stand five foot six, my voice, at least, is six foot five.

It would be my second trip to outpatient therapy that it was determined I could acquire a cane, and get off the crutches. It had not been eight months yet. And here I was, bearing full weight on a leg no one was certain I would walk on, without aid of crutches. The next time I visited Dr. Weiss, he was surprised.

"Very good. Already using a cane, huh? I'm impressed."

I loved defying my doctor's preconceived notions.

Over the next few weeks I attend therapy at Helen Hayes, and with Spring being here, I start to find time to be outdoors. Tori and Jillian and others continue to visit. I am still recovering.

In May we hit Memorial Day weekend, and I trek up to Albany for an event. I still cannot fence, but I can marshal, which I do. It was only a day trip, but once more I got to see a number of friends whom I'd not seen since my accident. Everyone was generally pleased to see me having recovered to the point I was already at so soon.

On my next visit to Dr. Weiss...he opted to remove my cast.

"You will need to have a brace made," he informed me. "But your leg is mostly healed, now."

Wow. It had been just shy of eight months since my accident, and already my leg was mostly healed, and I was on my feet again. I was walking. There was just one more thing.

"So, Dr. Weiss, can I have a note from you?"

"What kind of note?"

"Well, in order to begin fencing again, my friends have required me to get a Doctor's note."

"Can you fence left handed? I doubt you can hold up a blade properly in your right."

"Yeah, I can."

"Then you can fence."

"Okay, but I will still need a note, or they won't believe me."

"Sure."

He took out his prescription pad, and wrote me a note permitting me to begin fencing again.

Chapter 22 – En Guarde!

I had not fenced now since last November. Eight months. And I was still somewhat broken. The next Thursday night, I went to the church, and brought out my equipment. Bob was the first to meet me.

"I don't know, Will, did you get permission?"

Without hesitation, I presented Dr. Weiss' note.

"Well, then. Welcome back, buddy."

I don't know that I would call what I was doing fencing, per se. I was forced to work lefty, since my right bicep still refused to work, and of course, between the brace and the overall condition of my foot, my movement was more shuffling than stepping. But I was playing at fencing again.

I had not yet seriously considered returning to work. I was still injured. But I had acquired a lawyer, through my dad, and along the way some sort of settlement had been worked out, through my auto insurance. Yes, car insurance. Not medical. This whole thing fell under the uninsured motorist clause of my car insurance. They were covering the bulk of my medical bills. There was, apparently, with this money that would be mine, something beyond just coverage of my medical expenses, if the proper legal channels were surfed. So my lawyer did his part, and got me a small settlement. It was enough to cover my phone, cable, rent, and other essential bills for the time being. Since I was technically still injured. Returning to work had not even crossed my mind, yet.

Over the course of the month of July, I was able to reduce the wearing of my brace…until it became unnecessary. I was back on my own feet. I was walking with a limp, as predicted, but still not considered fully recovered. My right ankle did not bend correctly. In fact, I had a good twenty to thirty degree greater range of motion in my left than in my right, and my leg was an ugly, scarred mess.

Between the nasty looking skin graft, which flexed with my muscle and contorted to ugly shapes, and the scar of the bone graft running up the back of my leg nearly twelve inches, the right leg was not pretty. On top of that, it was still swollen above the ankle. They informed me it would likely be swollen like this for the rest of my life. To this day, I still refer to my right leg as the Leg of Doom™.

Then there was my arm. I had still not recovered the use of my right bicep. Whether muscle atrophy or unresolved nerve damage, still, I simply could not curl my bicep. This would make me somewhat crazy. I swear I spent hours staring at my arm, willing the damned bicep to curl. Willing does not make a thing happen.

Chapter 23 – A time to play, a time to laugh, a time to kill - kinda.

August rolled in and, with it, my most favorite annual SCA event. The Pennsic War was coming.

Pennsic XXIX, like the twenty-eight before, would draw over ten thousand SCAdians from around the world. I always enjoyed going to Pennsic. And this year would be my fifth.

Tori could not go. I was a bit disappointed about that, but it happened. So, for Pennsic, I would be on my own. How much trouble would I get into at Pennsic this time?

Pennsic is a world unto itself. Much like the advertising campaign for Las Vegas, a rule of thumb for Pennsic would be, "What happens at Pennsic War, stays at Pennsic War." My adventures at the Pennsic wars I have been to could be a story in-and-of themselves.

There are a number of important points one needs to know about Pennsic. I was told, at my very first war, back in 1996, that to truly experience this event, one must have three things happen. One, you need to get drunk. Two, you need to get wet during a rain because of a leak in your tent. Three, you need to get laid. As they say, "If you can't get laid at Pennsic, you can't get laid."

So, it can be quite the party. That is in addition to all the general socializing, fighting, fencing, archery, arts, sciences, music, dance and medieval shopping. It's an extravaganza of incredible proportions. I have had a good time at nearly every Pennsic I have attended. Fun with friends, fun fighting, flirting, and to be completely blunt, fucking. I have met a lot of neat people from all over the world, over the years, and continue to re-encounter them at the war. They have become friends, acquaintances, and comrades. All part of the fun.

Let me make one thing clear. I do not do one night stands. Now, this is not to say I have not had outright fuck buddies along the way. I think I might have mentioned I like sex. Possibly too much, but up to this particular point, I think I had accomplished all three prerequisites at each Pennsic.

So, here I was, largely recovered from my extensive injuries, and it was time, once again, to venture to Pennsylvania for the war. I was so jonesing to go, I am sure the vibrations of my excitement could have powered a large factory. I packed everything up, and started the six hour journey. Well, ok, to be fair, it should be closer to seven hours, but I am something of a lead foot. I can usually make it in six. Hey, I drive fast, but I don't weave and cut people off and act like a complete asshole on the road.

I think I save all my asshole tendencies for my relationships.

I get to Pennsic, and again feel as if I have returned home. I was still camping in the area known as the Bog with my first household. That group mostly camped and fought together. I didn't fight "heavy", of course, but since I was camping with them for the fifth time, I was accepted as a part of the house.

A quick digression. There are multiple combat arts practiced by participants in the SCA. In addition to fencing, and archery, which I have mentioned before, there is thrown weapons, equestrian activities, and heavy combat.

Heavy combat is the premier martial art of the SCA. This involves men and women donning armor, ranging from plastic to leather with plastic sewn in, to full metal plate, and heavy, steel helms are required. Their weapons are made of rattan, a wood similar to bamboo, but not hollow. Most blows are delivered to the head. Yeah, it's always sounded like an invitation for pain to me, too. Probably why I don't play that particular game.

Pennsic takes place at a large campground that the SCA takes over every August. I would guess that from my camp, up the hill to the rapier field near the top, is at least a quarter to a half a mile hike, which is even less fun when hauling a bag of fencing gear slung over your shoulder.

Last year I had gotten smart and acquired a rolling golf club cart to mount my bag on, to transport it up the damned hill. This year I would one-up that, and stow my gear at the top of the hill in my local shire's camp. Bob was camped there, so he had put up a small tent for supplies. That made life much easier.

Hard to believe that nine months after my accident, I was attending my regularly scheduled vacation. No, I still could not fence right-handed, and I was walking with a limp, but I was both walking *and* fencing - not too shabby.

I had made it to Pennsic. People were very glad to see me. And I was certainly glad to see them. I spent a bit more time in camp that year than previous years. Moving from one place to another was a lot more work now than it had been before. Yeah, I was without crutches or the cane, but I still had a limp, and I was still just a bit off.

I really enjoyed all the social contact at Pennsic. There's nothing like being surrounded by friends to make a person feel good.

Fencing was an interesting experience. First, I was only fighting with single sword, and as a lefty. I still had not gotten back any real use of my right arm. Yes, my fingers worked, and I could readily move from the shoulder, and even from the wrist, but I was still unable to curl my bicep with any weight. Ergo, fencing with a more-than-one but less-than-three pound sword was right out. Still, I made the best of it I could. I'd go up to the field, and take on challengers. I even had a few good fights.

One guy was a lot of fun, and I was having a very "on" day. I had probably gotten into that whole Zen zone business. At any rate, I was fighting well, and it was a good fight. When we were done, and removed our masks and got water, and we talked some.

"Not bad, man. That was fun," he complimented me.

"Yeah, it was, thanks," I replied.

"So like, you're from the East, right?"

"Yeah."

"Cool. They tell me there's this guy from the EK who is out here fencing, and like, apparently, less than a year ago, he was hit by a car, and they didn't know if he'd ever even walk again. If you know him, will ya point him out to me, so I can fence him."

"Hi, how ya doing?"

"What?"

"That would be me."

His reaction was really very neat. I love causing people to be stunned like that.

Later on at war, I had a similar conversation. There was another guy from another kingdom whom I kept trying to catch up with to fight. One of us always seemed to have a fight planned before we could catch one another, so we never managed to actually fight. After I had gotten particularly tired following a good bout, he found me again.

"Dude…I just found out what happened to you. Let me tell you…I'm scared of you now. I can't imagine what you were like when you were unhurt."

Damn did my ego appreciate that!

Of course, one interesting thing that kept happening was that I was getting much more sleep at odd times than usual. You see…I have never been a napper. I just don't like to take naps. I always figure if I nap, I get less sleep when I *need* to sleep. Always been that way. I have often been amazed at Tori's ability to nap whenever. How do people do that?

So I would, at a typical Pennsic, spend about two-thirds of the daylight hours up on the rapier field. I would fence, and marshal, and fence, and marshal, and usually fence some more. Then - more fencing.

Hell, the first time Tori and I attended Pennsic together, I had her in tow when I went up to the rapier field to only check the schedule. When I arrived our erstwhile Kingdom Marshal of Fence, or KMOF, the previously mentioned Jon, was with a friend of mine, Max. Max had been a marshal-in-training I had worked with for a while. I was only there to check our schedule, see if there were any times I needed to specifically be on the field.

"So, Max," Jon was saying. "I know you've been at it, so I wanted you to know that you are a marshal, now. Congrats. Anyhow, this gentleman over here is looking to authorize. Grab Will, there, and have at it, ok?"

My minute of checking the board turned into a twenty-minute authorization bout. Tori was none-too-happy with me on that one.

Anyhow, this Pennsic, post-injury, I found I would get easily fatigued. So I would go off to the side, near where my and my friends' gear had been set down, and I would lay down for a bit. I normally intended for it to be a brief respite, no more than a few minutes and, more than once, I dozed off completely.

I must have looked damned silly. Especially when I had my hat over my eyes to block the sun. At least once a day I dozed about fifteen to thirty minutes right there on the fencing field. Being injured sucks.

More than once, I surprised people with the drugs I was taking. Or rather, the drugs I was not taking. I had gone home from the rehab hospital with prescriptions for Oxycontin, Neurontin, and Percocet. Some very heavy narcotics in there. Over time, I had chosen to wean myself off of them. First was the Oxycontin. I just stopped taking it one day. Then, the Neurontin. Same thing. Last and not least, I stopped taking the Percocet. If I hurt, I relied on good old ibuprofen.

After my third surgery, on one visit to Dr. Weiss, he queried if I needed to refill the Percocet. I said, "No, sir. I have, like, sixty tablets still."

He found that pretty amazing. I told him I wasn't taking them, and he was even more surprised. When I told him I was just relying on ibuprofen, he asked how much? I told him only four-hundred milligrams, ergo two tablets. Again he had that very cool look of, 'no way, but go you!' I love that reaction.

So now that I was returning to fencing, Maren and Johan knew that it was my deepest desire to one day receive an OGR for my skill. And they knew that, now, I would be rebuilding almost from the ground up. So they offered to make me a cadet.

There are a number of student/mentor relationships in the SCA structure. The most well-known, even outside the medieval recreation world, is the knight/squire combo. A squire, as a student of the knight, learns from his teacher a number of things, in addition to good combat techniques, at least in theory. That is the most commonly found example even a non-SCAdian would know about. Then there are the service-award Peers, called Pelicans, and their students, protégés. The master teaches the student how to over-volunteer to help make the SCA run, and stuff like that. Those are the people without whom there would probably *be* no SCA. Ah, volunteer organizations. Next is the arts and sciences awarded Peers, called Laurels, and their students, apprentices. The student learns a craft from the teacher, usually, so they too may someday become a peer.

(Inserted digression: In 2015, the SCA added a new Peerage, for fencers: The Order of Defense. I could write an entire, probably biased history of the process that went into the making of this, but suffice it to say that has been an amazing addition to the game.)

Those are the four highest, Society-recognized awards of the SCA, the Peerages. A Knight, Pelican, Laurel or Master of Defense in any kingdom is still such in every other Kingdom. They are universal awards.

There are a number of awards below this, but this is not a story all about the SCA. Among these awards are the recipients of the Order of the Golden Rapier, called OGR, or their equivalents about the known world, (as well the rest of the SCA), including Bronze Rings, and more commonly White Scarves. The Dons and Doñas take on cadets, whom they are to pass their vast fencing knowledge on to, at least in theory. I was offered that chance to be a cadet to not one, but two OGRs, husband and wife. And I was crazy enough to accept. So, in their camp one afternoon, I formally took a scarf, and became their cadet. Now it's a question of who is crazier, them, or me?

Pennsic was winding down, and a tradition we had in our camp, on the second to last night of War, was the "eat it, drink it, burn it party." As we were all preparing to go home, there were consumables that had to be dealt with. So we could either eat it, drink it, or burn it. I had wanted to burn many things from my time of injury. First and foremost, the wheelchair. Of course, it had been rented, so I couldn't light it on fire. But damn did I want to!

When the guy came to pick-up the chair from my home, I told him how much I had wanted to launch it down the stairs, au flambé, but of course, that did not happen. Damn was I glad to be rid of that thing. I have a new respect for those who must spend their lives bound to those chairs. I don't envy any of you, but empathize with you.

There had been a rather cushy cushion for the wheelchair that I considered burning, but that just seemed gross - so, no. On the day of the party, I did find something to burn. I threw my temporary handicap permit into the fire.

Yes, it was still good for a few more months, but I did not need it. Rather than use it still, and deprive someone in far more need than I of good parking, it had to be destroyed. And more than that, I needed to burn something. Something had to be set on fire, like the phoenix of myth, in order to arise from the ashes. I simply needed to see the fire consume some aspect that represented this dark time of trial in my life. So there it was; the permit was the best item to serve that purpose.

I tossed that lovely little red pass, which had been hanging from my rearview mirror, into the fire. And I watched it ignite, and dissolve into flame. It felt good to see it go.

Chapter 24 – The candles seem to mean a lot more this time.

With Pennsic being over, it meant that summer was drawing to a close. But worse than that, it also meant my birthday was coming. On the one hand, it was something to look forward to. I have always liked my birthday. I enjoy the party, the thrill of friends and family celebrating as you turn a year older. On the other, I had to acknowledge just how dangerously close I had come this time to not getting here. I had almost expired before my twenty-eighth year.

Damn. Twenty-eight, and what did I have to show for it this year? Still single, I was with neither Tori nor Jill, though I still spent time with both on physical and intimate levels. As for a career? I was currently unemployed. But none of that mattered, I was still alive. Broken, yes, certainly, but still alive. And all my parts were my own, even if altered in various ways. So here I was, turning twenty eight. And it was not a bad thing.

It should probably be noted here that I have, over the course of my life, battled depression on and off. I was in and out of therapy throughout much of my formative years. My parents' divorce had really made a mess of my head, and I had other socialization issues that had made my life rough. As I got older, they got varied, and more complex. Now, of course, not long after arriving at the rehab hospital, they had had me pay a visit to the shrink.

Much to her surprise, I was coping extremely well. I have gotten good at telling a therapist that I want nothing to do with exactly what they want to hear, but, truth be told, I was coping well. I chose the sunny side. I chose to fight hard. I chose to accept what happened, and not be broken up about it. I saw no point in being pained and saddened by my situation, when I could continue to work on my recovery and push as hard as possible.

Even now, ten months or so later, I was still doing ok. Sure, there were things I wanted to make happen, but all in all, I was doing OK, day to day. Things just sort of went along for the next month or so. Of course, things never stay status quo in my life, in any way, for long.

My friend Carl had married his wife Angela while they were in their early twenties. He had knocked her up, after all, but they seemed to have a good, loving relationship. Carl was, to all intents and purposes, my fencing student. I had taught him the basics, and spent the past year or so teaching him beyond that. In my absence, Johan had taken over one of my practices, while Maren ran the other for me.

Now that I was returning to fencing, Carl wanted to be along with me again. So we were going to hit the Wednesday practice that was not local. Carl and Angela had met me at a local mall, and were going to follow me south to the practice. I had a video tape I needed to drop off at Tori's, and it was more-or-less along the way. So we would swing by there first, then head to practice.

Rolling along route 17 in north Jersey can be an experience. It is a two or three lane divided highway, depending on where exactly you are. There are businesses all along the road, so traffic can get rather hairy, as people pull in and out of those places.

I could go into a long rant here about New Jersey drivers. Hey, I grew up in the Midwest, and learned to drive there. People are simply more courteous. For example, they don't take a turn signal as a warning that they need to cut someone off, they see it as a courteous gesture. There are three particular maneuvers that are almost unique to New Jersey, if not in their existence, then in the frequency of their occurrences. The first I call the "New Jersey Left." This maneuver occurs when the light turns green, and the first car at the light makes a swift left turn, before oncoming traffic can cross the intersection. The second maneuver is the "swerve-turn." This is a swerve right to turn left, swerve left to turn right. Like you are on a bicycle or something, rather than driving a one, or two plus, ton automobile. Often times, those are done in a slow manner that prevents a driver from passing someone turning against busy, oncoming traffic, which makes it even more infuriating. Last, and certainly not least, is the inconvenient turn. Let's say I am traveling down the street, and there are no cars behind me. That is when you turn from an intersecting street in front of me, even though you could wait three to five seconds and get behind me, since no one else is there. But then, as if this isn't annoying enough, the driver is traveling at a speed about a third of what you were going, and isn't accelerating. What the fuck is that about?

But I digress. This, too, could make another unique side story.

So there we are, me in my shiny black Celica, Carl and Angela and their son a few cars behind me, traveling along route seventeen. And, as happens from time to time, the highway comes to a dead stop. I have paid attention, and stop well shy of the Ford Excursion in front of me. I was on my mobile phone, chatting with Tori, informing her that I was, in fact, bringing that tape to her place. I had no hands-free device, no laws had yet been passed about that.

It was completely unexpected. Suddenly, I feel as if someone has punched me in the jaw. And I lurched forward, and the car is filled with a fine smoke. What the fuck? Not punched in the jaw, my airbag has been deployed. My front end and the rear of the Excursion have been merged. And where is my fucking mobile phone, anyhow? Then I notice, hey, crap, the passenger airbag has shattered my windshield. It's all spider-webbed. Wild.

"I'm okay," I shout out into my car, hoping Tori can still hear me, wherever the hell the mobile had been sent. "The airbag knocked the phone out of my hand, but I am fine!"

Carl is there, and has yanked open my door.

"Dude, you alright?" he asked, concerned.

"Yeah, I'm okay," I say, arising.

Yup, nothing hurt. Well, just a small cut on the tip of a finger, I'm betting that's from the shattered windshield.

"What the fuck was that?"

"The asshole behind you didn't stop, and plowed you into the truck. You sure you're not hurt?"

"Yeah, yeah, just surprised."

We get the cars off the road, and I see that my assailant, an early nineties Nissan Sentra, has a somewhat crunched front end. But his car is still drivable. The Excursion has a small scratch on the bumper - barely even noticeable. But my Celica, well, she's an accordion now.

Damn.

I find my mobile, and let Tori know where I am, and what has happened, but that I am totally fine.

The cops have arrived, and the passenger of the Excursion claims that her neck is bothering her. So of course, they need to call in the paramedics. Well, shit. I'm ok. How come she thinks she's hurt?

They arrive, they see the wreckage of my poor car, and talk to the injured woman. I am just in earshot of that.

"Okay, so you were in the Celica, there, right?"

"Oh, no, I was in the truck."

"Oh."

They turned to the nearest cop, "Who was in that one?"

They point to me, and the paramedics suddenly are far more interested in me than her.

"Are you okay, sir?"

"Yeah, fine, thanks."

"No, really, are you sure you're okay?"

"Yeah. Just a little cut from the windshield, but it's minor."

"Will you sign this waiver, that you are refusing medical treatment?"

"Sure."

So I sign, and they go.

I think when she saw the ambulance, Torrance may have nearly lost it. She thought, before she noticed me standing there, that I had lied about my latest incident. My car is not so hot. I am, just fine.

But damn...I loved that stupid car. And that would be the end of my Celica. My favorite car ever, a sleek little black two door coupe. She had over one-hundred and thirty thousand miles on her odometer, and this was her second major accident. I had to total my poor car.

Hey, let's face it...I am a guy. I love cars. Nope, can't break 'em down, repair or rebuild 'em, but I am fond none-the-less. The Celica had only been my third car. Before, I had owned a 1984 Subaru GL, and after that a piece-of-shit Plymouth Laser. But the Celica was the sweetest of them all, and her demise made me very sad.

The bout with the Excursion led me to a conclusion: No more small cars. It was time for an SUV. But most were too large, or ugly, or gas guzzling. So where would I turn? Toyota provided the answer for me. Their engineers chose that year to redesign the RAV4, and I really liked what they came up with. My mind was made up before I even entered the dealership to take a test drive.

Of course, it took a month to get the RAV with exactly the toys I wanted. It had to be black, and I had to have manual transmission again.

Yup, I can be a spoiled child sometimes. Hey, if it's my ride, I want it like I want it, why choose from a lack of decent choices just for the sake of having a car to drive?

A rental car for all that time would have sucked but, fortunately for me, Tori's older sister had a car that was just sitting around unused, and she let me borrow it. That made life so very much easier.

That was not, in any way, shape, or form, my first car accident. My first car, my Subaru, I had side-swiped another car with, sliding on some ice, in the winter. My second car, my Laser, got driven across an uneven field. Hey, I had a choice between the oncoming traffic of a two-lane highway in upstate New York, or the open field. The field won, my car, not so much. Damaged the subframe. What is the deal with me and cars? Was I an unlucky car designer in a past life or something?

Chapter 25 – No rest for the weary.

I was now mostly recovered. I was still going to outpatient therapy at Helen Hayes, and they were doing a number of different things to improve my dexterity, my ability to use my right arm, and my walking. All things considered, I was moving along swimmingly.

I had demanded way back in July hydrotherapy. I had both heard and read that time working on atrophied muscles in water was a fantastic way to recover. So I pushed to make that happen. I didn't want to just regain the use of my damaged body parts, I wanted them as close to the way they used to be as possible.

So, in the water, they had me walk, and do all kinds of motions with my arm. I think it might have been while in the water that I first regained movement of my right bicep. It can be so totally frustrating to stare at your arm, will it to move, and have nothing happen. But I was not willing to quit. I think my therapists had gotten used to all the old folks they worked on, and the constant whining that would ensue. Often, those people had a low tolerance for pain and strain, so they would do a lot of complaining. Me? I practically asked for more. Often the questions went as follows:

"That hurt?"

"Yup."

"Want to stop?"

"Nope."

"You sure?"

"Yup."

And so on.

Another therapy they wanted to do was electro-shock. No, they didn't hook electrodes to my poor brain, though in many respects that might not have been a bad idea. No, they hooked electrodes to my atrophied right leg, and sent waves in to force the muscles to do something. That would, at least in theory, give me more bend in my ankle. It would increase my range of motion, and allow me to walk with a more normal gait. At least in theory.

As the months marched on, somehow, I was beginning to walk without the limp. That was technically not possible. My tibia and fibula are fused and, therefore, do not move in the correct manner that should allow me to walk without limping. In addition to that, the swelling of my ankle, and the reduction in range of motion, should not allow me to walk normally. According to medical science, I should not be capable of walking without a limp. Yet, as therapy wore on, and the days and months moved ahead, my walk became less shuffled, and my limp began to go away.

My family had been very supportive in all of this. They'd been there for me. Dad and Lucy would check on me frequently, mom would call often, and my sister even checked in. My friends had also been there for me. Between Bob stopping in constantly, and my other SCA friends making a point of seeing how I was doing, I was never alone. I always had cheerleaders willing me to recover.

I have often remarked that the mind is the most powerful healing tool we have. Our real limits are only in our hearts and heads. If one believes that one can make a recovery from a crippling injury, one can. If one shunts positive energy into the healing process, believes there are no limits, then there are no limits. Sure, that's crazy talk, to some folks. I mean, c'mon, what's next, crediting God and angels and such? Now I am not saying that there are not higher powers out there and effecting the universe continually, but I am saying that we have a great deal more power in our own selves than we usually take credit for.

I think this is a perfectly acceptable location to digress and insert a rant.

There is a movement in modern America to equate three separate, though largely equal tenets as one, and this particular notion makes me nuts, sometimes. These tenets are religion, spirituality, and morality. The Religious Right wants us to understand that if you are not religious, you can be neither spiritual nor moral.

That is bullshit.

The three tenets are separate and, in many ways, equal. It is very possible to be any one alone, or any combination of all three. One can be religious, but spiritual and amoral. One can be moral, but not spiritual nor religious, and one can be spiritual, but have no religion nor morals. Why do these things so often get tied together, when they are so vastly different?

Over the years I have tried to take part in religion. I was raised Jewish and, while I still relate to my heritage, and still completely respect and appreciate the faith of my upbringing, I have found that the fundamental underpinnings of organized religion no longer resonate in me. Before I met Tori, I was not much of a spiritual man. I did not have any real beliefs, per se, and, while I vaguely believed in a higher power of some sort, there was just not much to be added to the topic. Through Torrance, I saw a new philosophy, and discovered my spiritual side. As to morals, well I believe that morality is an individual thing, as are all these tenets. My moral code is not going to be the same as anyone else's, really. I am who I am, and I believe what I believe, and what I consider right and wrong are going to be vastly different than what any other liberal will think, and even more different than what any conservative would consider.

That's not to say that there are not certain things that simply are moral versus immoral. Killing humans for sport is amoral. Stealing for profit is not moral. But, of course, as with much of life, there are gray areas. Stealing to feed your hungry family is not necessarily right, but neither is it wrong, if you save a life that way. Killing to defend your own life when attacked is still not right, but not a premeditated wrong, and so on. Too many people want to see the world in extremes, black and white, right and wrong, good and evil. Trouble is, very little of the world is on the ends of the extremes. Most of the world falls into the gray shades or colors between the extremes.

I have never understood what comfort people take in seeking those extremes. I live much of my own existence in many of the greys, so is it just that I accept the extremes are, well, extreme, or am I missing something else? So ends this digression. We now return you to our story, already in progress.

They said it would take one to three years before I'd walk. It took a bit more than seven months. They said my right arm may never work again. Well, yes, it was taking what seemed like forever, but it was working now. And they told me I would walk with a limp for the rest of my life. Somehow, I am managing to walk that limp off.

I believe that I can recover. Completely. Totally. That is what I focused on.

My relationships with Tori and Jill remained complex. I spent a lot of time with Tori, whenever I could. She was my best friend, and knew me more than anyone. Save one secret, my relationship with Jillian. I didn't know why, at the time, I still had my secret little thing with Jill. I didn't know if it was because she made me feel good, made me feel something beyond pain and discomfort, or if there was something deeper. It's kind of amazing what we see in hindsight, really. Jill loved me. I did not see it for what it was at the time, of course, but she did. So did Tori, but I was missing that, too.

All either of them wanted from me was love in return. And while I could give them something akin to love, it was not, I know now, love itself. Actually, it kind of was, but I certainly did not see it for what it was until it was far too late. Tori never gave up on me. She was always there. She helped me get better. She made sure that I was never really alone. Guess what I am going to completely fuck up soon.

Chapter 26 – To see, or not to see, that is the question.

Near the end of October, I opted for yet another surgery. This time it was totally voluntary. I wanted to have my eyes shot. Lasik, laser eye treatments, had been around for a good five years, or so, at this point, and I know, longer, when you take the research time into account. Back in February Tori had taken me to a place for a consultation. And the first place I went to made a point of stating that I had over-sized pupils. OK, great, so what? Well, since my pupils were so big, the chances of my having glare and halo and night-vision issues following Lasik were about ten percent higher, but they still wanted to schedule the procedure.

I went to a different place for a consultation, and they told me the same thing about my over-sized pupils, but they then offered a different plan.

"In six months the FDA will be approving a new software for this procedure. With that, the risk factor will be eliminated. If you wait, we will call you."

Works for me.

So they called, and I went.

Lasik surgery is a freaky experience. First, you are awake for the whole thing. Second, your eyes are open.

They told me, "Stare at the laser, that will improve the correction."

I stared at the beam in my eye. The first eye was freakier than the second, but I think that's largely because the valium hadn't fully kicked in.

Recovery was a bit uncomfortable, but there was really no pain. The next day, I was seeing twenty-thirty in one eye, twenty-forty from the other. In the next week, my vision improved to twenty-twenty plus in one eye, twenty-twenty minus in the other.

I had worn glasses since the fourth grade. It has thus been eighteen years with nearly Coke-bottle bottom lenses. I had gotten my first pair of contact lenses just before my thirteenth birthday. My grandpa paid for them after I met his challenge, and lost about fifteen pounds.

I digress, of course.

Are you familiar with the stupid weight yo-yo? All my life I have been overweight. Sometimes more, sometimes less, but never where I should be. I always carried extra weight on my body somewhere, and it had been a constant struggle. My first real push to diet, since my teen years, was in 1997. That followed a very unpleasant incident at the Las Vegas airport.

***

It was, pretty much, my first real job out of college. I had only been working for the company I was with for a month or so. Being the nature of the business we were in, we attended the monstrous Consumer Electronics Show in Las Vegas. That show, held annually, features the latest and greatest in, well as the title implies, consumer electronics. It was me, the owner of the company, his Vice President, and his Business Manager visiting Vegas. Ergo, the entirety of the company. We stayed, during this trip, at the MGM Grand hotel. There was nothing special about the place; the rooms we had were dry, and not anything to write home about. Not bad, but I don't doubt they have better places in Sin City.

I have never been much of a gambler, so aside from the occasional coin in the slots, the allure passed swiftly. Anyhow, we did our thing, and then packed it all up. We had traveled as a group, the whole company.

For the return trip home, I was ready to go to the airport, but the other guys were running late, taking their time doing whatever-the-hell it was they were doing. We finally got to the airport, with only a short period of time to spare. We were totally going to miss our plane. It was already mostly boarded by the time we were checking our bags. Not good.

So, we got to airport security. The other guys got through, and raced for the plane. For some reason, the security people decided to do a thorough search through my bag.

You're kidding, right guys?

Oh no, they did a thorough search. I don't even know what for, and the clock was ticking. Mind you, this was years before "nine-eleven" changed the way security is handled in American airports. Finally they let me go. I repacked my bag as quick as I could, and I ran for the gate.

Now, of course, as if the added drama were necessary, our gate was at the far end of the terminal.

So I ran the best I could. I managed to arrive as they were closing the door to the gate. Thanks, guys, for holding the plane for me. No, really. You'd think my co-workers might have mentioned to someone, maybe, that I was still coming. Guess not.

I got aboard, and I could not catch my breath. We took off, and I still could not catch my breath. We flew over the Midwest, and I had only just begun to catch my breath.

That was unacceptable. I couldn't believe I was in that bad of shape.

I joined a gym, pretty much, that next Monday. And then I altered my diet. Round one of dozens, of course. So began another yo-yo cycle.

Tori and I met the next year, in the spring of 1998. I had dropped a lot of weight at that point, but somewhere in the course of the next year, I picked it back up again.

There is a line in a song by Barenaked Ladies that goes something like, "I'm like a baby, she's like a cat, when we are happy, we both get fat." That may be why I found my weight increasing again.

So, I had just begun to get my diet and exercise back under control when, wham, I meet a car, while on foot

I've been telling you this story here.

Since I was not really eating much for the first month after my accident, I had shed some weight. Not a diet plan I would recommend, though. Of course, I had considered penning a diet of that nature. But somehow the "Car Shock – Get Injured to Lose Weight" diet program just didn't seem like it would be a great plan for everyone. Then I considered the lawsuits from those who got it wrong, and were more severely wounded, or died.

Of course, that would have been an interesting study of Darwinism in action. I mean, c'mon, how many morons would I have taken out of the gene pool attempting to follow such a stupid diet plan?

Brrreeeeeeeeeep! You, over there...yeah, you! Get out of the gene pool!

Let's face it. This pool seriously needs more chlorine sometimes.

Chapter 27 – Amazing what a man will do for a nice set of boobs.

Tori continued to be there for me, and while I thought we simply had a fantastic friendship going, she was hiding her true feelings for me. Truth be told, she wasn't hiding her feelings for me; I was just too dumb to see it for what it was. That would come out in November.

It was a normal SCA meeting at the church. The usual suspects were all there, and nothing out of the ordinary was planned. Then, she walked in. Now, as much as most folks have never believed me, it was not her incredible breasts that caught my eyes first. Yup, they were certainly impressive, but they were not what drew me to her. It was also not her golden blonde hair, either. Long, flowing, pure blonde, cascading down her shoulders et cetera, et cetera. Nope, that wasn't what got me, either. It was her eyes. The greenest, most penetrating eyes I had ever seen. That was not the first time I had seen those eyes. I had seen them before in my dreams.

Now, some who know me know that I do not normally dream. It is a very rare occurrence when I do. But in my youth, when I believe I dreamed more often, I am pretty certain that I had seen those eyes before. I am a romantic at heart. That is probably why I play in an organization that emphasizes the romanticized aspects of chivalry. I have long believed in the idea of the one true love. And long believed that when she came into my world, I would just know. No questions, no debate, I would simply know.

Those eyes. That hair. And yes, admittedly, those breasts, I thought, holy shit, is this her? It was precisely the one year anniversary of my accident.

I believe in karma, to a large degree, and I believed that this was my karmic repayment for my suffering. Her name was Rachel, and not surprisingly, we hit it off right from the start.

Tori was initially very supportive of this situation. She told me to pursue it, to see where it might lead. Since Jill was totally on the down-low to begin with, she also accepted my need to pursue this.

It started out slowly enough. We chatted on the internet, we spoke on the phone. And then it began to involve more time with her, and we progressed from simply talking to hanging out to making out in a matter of days.

Tori would call, and I would tell her I was busy. In fact, I inadvertently found myself blowing Tori off to be with Rachel. Out of the blue, I was spending an awful lot of time and effort on Rachel. And Tori was sort of shunted to the back of my mind.

Not fair of me, I know, and yes, I recognize what an asshole this makes me sound like. You can't say anything bad about me I've not already considered. Then it turned ugly. Suddenly, Torrance made it clear she did not approve of this situation. She did not appreciate my blowing her off for that girl.

Now I was really confused. Hadn't she told me to go ahead and pursue it in the first place? There was a confrontation I only remember hazily. I am pretty certain I strove to block much of it from my mind. Tori proceeded to confess her love for me. And I just stood there, stunned. Torrance actually got so emotional, so angered by my lack of response, that she pushed me into a wall. She told me I had to make a choice. I either dropped Rachel, or dropped her.

Tori had been there through thick and thin. She had helped to nurse me back to health. She had been the best friend I had ever had, on levels I could only begin to fathom. Rachel was new in my life. She was beautiful, and she was intelligent. And I was still absolutely convinced that she was The One. The romanticized soul mate I had been waiting for. I left Tori's apartment. I chose Rachel.

Take a moment. I know that seems drastically unfair of me. How could I choose this new girl over the woman who had been there for me? But then, by the same token, how could I have been involved with her and Jillian also? What the fuck was my problem? Yes, I don't deny that I was a real asshole. I wanted too badly to believe in true love.

Rachel practically lived with me. She was, after all, living at home with her parents. She would spend about five nights a week with me. I even let her claim a couple drawers in my dresser. We were inseparable. We hit SCA events together. We showered together. We talked on the phone when we were apart. The month of December was probably the most intense relationship I had ever had. I learned how to share my bed with someone. Sex had never been an issue, but the cuddling and sharing a bed all night had never been something I had been comfortable with before, but with Rachel, it was a constant state of things.

For Hanukkah, Rachel wrapped herself in a bow. And that was all. We had a lot of fun.

New Year's Eve rolled along, and we both went to the party at Chris'. There were a number of friends there, and we played silly games, and Chris of course took numerous photos of it all. It stunned me to see just how fat I had become. Damn, had I gotten heavy.

It wasn't long after New Years I started to notice a void in my life, and that I began to miss Tori.

Chapter 28 – I realize I am a great big jerk, Part I.

Before Rachel, Tori and I had spoken at least two or three times a day. No one knew me like Tori did. No one had been there for me like she had. It had been more than a month since we'd spoken. For that first month, Rachel filled all those voids, but something was beginning to be missing. Something was starting to feel - disconnected.

For the first time since my accident, I started up working with a temp agency. Nothing too thrilling, but at least I was beginning to work again, but I was more and more feeling this void, this emptiness. What was going on?

My contact, beyond just Tori, with people overall was less. Deb was not speaking to me, either. Tori had loosed a lot of venom, and a number of people were siding with her, and avoiding me. Suddenly, several of the friends who had been there were turning their backs on me. I was so blinded by the large breasted blonde and her green eyes that it was being completely missed by me. Increasingly, I felt a bizarre sense of loneliness. What the fuck? Why was I feeling alone?

Then, one night, it hit me. I was lying beside Rachel, naked, and holding her. And suddenly, I understood. I was holding her. She was not touching me. I would caress her, stroke her, hold her. And she did not reciprocate.

I mentioned it to her one night. How I felt empty. Her response?

"Well, you shouldn't go straight for the clitoris every time."

What? Now wait a minute, since when do I go straight for the clitoris?

Okay, this is probably going to be a massive overshare, but it's rather necessary to explain some things about me. I am a huge fan of not sex, and an enormous fan of foreplay. I believe very much that the first erogenous zone on a woman is her mind. Then, all of her body follows. Yup, the whole body can be stimulated, if you take the time to do that. I have always really enjoyed taking the time to do that. I love the female body. Probably too much, sometimes.

I was feeling increasingly alone, even when lying naked beside my girlfriend. And it wasn't just that she was not touching me physically, I don't believe she was touching me emotionally anymore, either.

I had a Friday night alone one time, and went to Bob's place. I was finding that I found I wanted less and less time with Rachel. For the most part we were still doing okay, or so I let myself believe, but it was feeling more and more awkward. More than anything, I really wanted to talk to Tori. But I was not about to call her, she made it very clear that once my choice was made, it was done and over.

Most Friday nights at Bob's place we worked on projects, mostly assembling armor for SCA combat. We were all there doing our thing. Painting was happening, the heavy fighter guys were building new armor pieces. I may have been building new bucklers for fencing. We started to talk, and I began to express my increasing discontent with my relationship. Leave it to Bob to say the best one-liners.

"So it sounds like you are telling me that your bank account is going down on you faster than she is?"

Dude. Whoa.

Truth be told, it wasn't entirely untrue. I would buy her gifts, take her out to dinner, drive her all around, and seldom did she pay, or even offer. So, yes, that was where the situation seemed to be headed. What the fuck?

Valentine's Day came. I hate Valentine's Day. Doesn't matter if I am seeing someone, or not. I hate that ludicrous Hallmark™ holiday. I blame my mother.

My mother's very favorite holiday of them all is Valentine's Day. For her, it's a second Hanukkah. We would often have a party on Valentine's Day. Mom made sure gifts were passed out. She made a huge to-do of it. I grew to despise that holiday. Especially because more often than not, I was single when it rolled along.

Valentine's Day to me has always been Black Insert-the-day-of-the-week-here. Even when I was seeing someone, I loathed this holiday. I still do. I probably always will. I know what you're thinking, "And yet you call yourself a romantic."

Rachel and I did something or other. I honestly cannot remember what, exactly, we did to celebrate. But there was one thing that stuck out in my mind. We did not have sex. When you are in a relationship with someone, let's be blunt. There are certain times when lovemaking is a given. Birthdays, Christmas, New Years, and Valentine's Day. If you are with someone, and you have a sexual relationship, of course, you get it on, on those holidays. Right?

We didn't. No sex. We simply went to bed. No cuddling that night, either. What was going on here? My discontent was growing. I was feeling increasingly alone. Even with my girlfriend lying beside me. Why? What had gone wrong?

I wanted desperately to talk to Tori. Suddenly I was missing her very much.

I dared not call her. I knew she would never take my call.

And then an event popped up. There was an annual event in the Barony to the south, and I knew she would be there. And she was.

Chapter 29 – I know I am a great big jerk, Part II. Just to reiterate the point.

I didn't know how to do it. I went to the event to fence, and Rachel was there, but I was distracted. I wanted to seek out and speak with Tori. As the event was winding down, I found her in the parking lot.

"Tori?"

"I don't have anything to say to you."

"I really miss talking to you. I, really would like to talk to you."

"Yeah? Well you should have chosen wiser, then."

I don't remember the rest of that conversation, but we wound up in a shouting match in the parking lot after that. I have no idea how it ended, or what all was said, just that it left me feeling even more awful. I drove home with Rachel, and somehow convinced her to let me have the night to myself.

I was truly alone. And feeling totally miserable. I suspect many of you are probably thinking I got what I deserved for leaving Tori like I did. You may be right.

It had been more than a year since my accident, and I was fully recovered, physically. On my last visit to see Dr. Weiss, he had made me walk away from him, then back towards him.

He shook his head at that. "Well, okay, that's impossible. Not bad."

We talked some more, and this was the last thing he said to me:

"Ok, Warren, normally I don't say this, because it is over-optimistic. But I will say it to you anyhow. You will fully recover. In time you will get back all the sensation and use in your arm, and you will be whole. I put you together good, but you healed beautifully. Good luck."

I never have seen Dr. Weiss since. Read some about him, know that he worked on a pro-athlete or two along the way. But that was my last time seeing him.

I survived getting hit by a car while on the street. I had recovered beyond where I was expected to, far faster than I had been expected to. I had come a very long way. So why was I still feeling so miserable? How had it come to this? How was I so totally and completely alone?

Rachel, I had believed she was my ideal, and I turned my back on a lot of people to be with her. I had given up the best friend I had ever had to be with her, and what good had that done me?

For the first time in my life, I was somewhat suicidal. It wasn't serious, and the thought of ending my own life was immediately followed by another intruding thought, telling me to shut the fuck up and deal. It was not an out I could or would take. This was the absolute lowest I had ever felt in my life. I slept even more poorly than normal that night.

That Sunday morning after the event, when I got out of bed, I remained quiet and in silence, feeling my misery. The phone rang.

"Hello?"

"Warren? It's Tori. Let's talk."

My heart skipped a beat or two. We talked. A lot. About a lot of different things. In time, I got on the road, and drove to her apartment. Tori let me in. And she held me. I cried. A lot.

"I knew that this was my one chance to reach you," she told me. "I saw in the lot yesterday that you were nearly gone, totally lost, and as much as a part of me wanted to let you suffer, I couldn't. I guess I still care too much."

"Thank you."

We talked a lot that day, and I decided that it was time to end my relationship with Rachel.

I suck at ending relationships nearly as much as I suck at being in them in the first place. I tried to find the right time. I was encouraged and discouraged by Tori at the same time. She threatened to stop talking to me again if I didn't put an end to my relationship. I took Rachel to dinner. And I finally let it out.

"Rachel…this isn't working."

"What's that?"

"This. Our relationship. It's just not working."

"Warren, I love you."

"Do you? How come I don't feel it?"

We talked in a lot of circles that night. And rather than sway me to give her another chance, to keep at the relationship, she managed to convince me that it was absolutely time that I end it. We went back to my place, and I asked her to gather up her stuff, get packed. I think I was heading to fencing practice, and told her I would get my key from her later.

Rachel should have been an actress. The performance she put on was an Oscar worthy drama. She cried. She sobbed. She collapsed at the foot of my bed, as she attempted to gather the ridiculous amount of stuff she had left in my apartment.

I was feeling more angry than upset over the performance she was putting on, and finally left to go to fencing. I have no memory of this part, but I got a call as I was leaving practice. It was not Rachel, it was Jillian.

"What's up?"

"Your girlfriend called me. So you dumped the bitch, huh?"

"What did she say?"

"She's a wreck. She wanted my sympathy as she was packing her shit. She kept collapsing, she claimed. She was so torn up by your rejection."

"You're not serious?"

"Oh yeah."

"She's still there, isn't she?"

"Probably. I'm sure she passed out again."

"Oy."

Yup, sure enough, I found her passed out amongst her stuff on my floor.

Give me a break.

I didn't feel like being a total ass. So I let her sleep on the futon in the living room that night. I was not at all about to entertain the notion of being with her any more. She showed me I was right to close that door. Rachel left the next morning.

Chapter 30 – Sometimes I do make the right choice.

It was over. But I still felt pretty empty.

The coming weekend had been a trip we'd planned. King's and Queen's rapier champions. The tourney would be up in Vermont. Yes, it was early March, but that is where we would be. Rachel and I had gotten a hotel room for this event. But I would now be going alone.

"So you ended it?" Tori questioned me on the phone later.

"Yes."

"And she took all her stuff?"

"Not all of it, no."

"Why not?"

"She was too broken up to collect it all."

"Give me a break! So you'll just toss it out?"

"No. I will get it to her."

"So you aren't actually done with her, then?"

"Yes I am."

"If you still have her stuff, no you aren't."

Torrance was angry with me when I left for Vermont that Friday night.

The event site for the tourney was behind high snow banks. We had to drag our gear over them to get into the church, where we would be fighting.

I didn't think. I just fought my bouts. We fought in round-robin pools of about eight fencers each. In a round-robin, you fight everyone in your pool, and generally the top two combatants advance to the next round. In my pool, I only lost one fight.

I advanced to the second round.

That was the first time I had done that. It was very cool. I didn't get much further. But to have come that far, a year after being so badly broken, I was totally pleased.

Friends received awards at court that night. Then, back at the hotel, we gathered in a room, and drank, and had some great conversations. For the first time in weeks, I was neither lonely, nor sad. This trip turned out to be just what I needed.

When I got home, I made arrangements to get the rest of Rachel's stuff to her. We would meet at the mall she worked at. Arrangements were made, and we met in the lot. I passed her the box of stuff that she had left in my place. I expected her to make a scene. But she didn't, and that was a good thing. She handled it all much more calmly, and took her stuff.

We actually continued to speak for some time after that. She started to see another guy from the local group. I knew they had gotten together immediately after our break up. Initially, I presumed she'd started sleeping with him right away. We all learned, as he complained loudly, that in fact she refused to sleep with him. I know for certain that he spent far, far more money on her than I ever did. In time she agreed to be his girlfriend. Yet we all still heard about how she would not sleep with him. But they were together, and that was enough for him.

Rachel rode out with him to Pennsic that year. They'd been together for over five months, and yet she had not slept with him. Funny that, she and I had had sex within a couple of weeks of meeting. She infuriated him with her attitude once they got to Pennsic. Rachel attended her first Pennsic for a whopping fifty hours or so. And in those fifty hours, after five months with that guy and no sex, she screwed two guys she met randomly at the War.

How come I know this? Well, I was walking back to camp from fencing in the woods. I encountered a disheveled Rachel, attending the embers of a dying fire. She had a look about her.

"Having fun?" I asked.

"Uh huh," she replied.

"So…did someone get laid?" I could just tell. Rachel didn't respond, she just got all coy and cutesy. "You did, didn't you?"

"Yeah," she admitted. "It was awesome."

The guy who brought her to Pennsic, her "boyfriend", had had enough. He abandoned her, literally, and she had to find a different ride home. I learned she slept with him, too, as payment for the ride. I felt even better about not being with her.

Blinded. I still cannot believe, years later, how blind I had been. Amazing what a good set of tits, amazing eyes and nice hair will do to a man.

Chapter 31 – Welcome to AA – Assholes Anonymous.

Tori and I began our friendship again. But it was different. She acted differently toward me, in many ways. I didn't fully understand it, but neither did I question it. We were friends again, and that meant the world to me.

Other friends, however, who had sided with Tori during my relationship with Rachel, were loath to take me back. Even though Torrance and I were friends again, and speaking publicly, there were others who were much colder to me now. Deb, for example, grew increasingly distant. There were numerous times at SCA meetings, on Thursdays, where I felt increasingly ostracized. So how do you atone for being an asshole?

How does one convince people that one accepts one did something wrong? How do you get people to take you back? The problem here is in caring what other people think. Yes, it is good to have friends, and to have people care about you. But the danger is in caring too much about how people think about you. When you care too much about what you show to them, you might just lose a few pieces of yourself along the way. Little did I know, that's what I was, and had been doing.

I was still depressed. Still didn't have a job. And while Tori and I were friends again, I still was feeling alone. Not for the first time, I went into therapy. I sought out the roots of my depression. I determined that I was usually treating the symptoms, but not the cause. There had to be something I was missing, or else why did I keep missing it?

I determined, after a few weeks of therapy, that the root of it all was fear. I had never considered myself to be afraid of anything. I always felt that I had no fear. That is a stupid thing to believe. What I feared was failing. Because of that fear, I often did not try. If I don't try, I cannot fail. Of course, conversely, I cannot succeed, either. Turns out I was equally fearing success.

I went to college and got a degree in Theatre. I worked in professional theatre for how long? Practically not at all. In part that was due to a fear to try, and in part, it was because I discovered I was not nearly cut-throat enough to step on all the right people to necessarily get anywhere in the theatre world.

Radio: I had loved my time as a DJ in college. I practically lived at the college station. I had made some attempts after college to get into professional radio. But rather than search every classic rock station in every itty-bitty market throughout the country, I wanted to stay in Ithaca, or the northeast at least. I wanted to keep near friends. So, rather than put my tapes out there, all across the country, to get a radio job, I gave up when I failed at finding work in New York somewhere.

Writing: I wrote my first fifty-page illustrated story when I was nine. It was relatively complex, and I am glad that no child psychologist got ahold of it, because they might well have locked me up. I did, after all, kill off all the adults in the world in this story. I had been writing on and off, in fits and starts, for years. I had begun a story during one of my duller jobs, and eventually it evolved into the quintet of novels I plotted out. I completed the first and second books, and tried to find an agent - half-heartedly. And what do you know, I still write. If you are reading these words, then you are obviously aware of that fact. But I never pursued publishing in any fantasy magazines, or journals, or even online. I wanted to succeed, and feared that nearly as much as I feared failing.

Most glaring of all is my continued failure at relationships. Before Rachel, there was Tori, before Tori, there was a girl named Carrie, before Carrie there was Shelly, and so on. I was never able to fully commit, never able to say "I love you." I was barely able to express real emotions. I was so afraid of doing to my own non-existent children what was done to me that I just could not get committed to anyone.

A necessary digression here, since my mom and dad may well read this. I love them both, and they never treated me poorly. I was in no way abused or truly neglected. However, being emotionally sensitive, I took their divorce hard and blamed myself. I just could not see putting my own possible children through the same emotional wringer.

Anyhow, I was seeking some intangible thing, that I presumed I would simply know upon its finding. Yet, I never did find it. Always, I looked, constantly tried, and constantly failed. It all boiled down to fear.

I looked at my situation with a fresh eye, and then I looked at my own family. My dad is on anti-depressants. My grandmother is as well. My mom probably should be. Well fuck. What does that tell you?

Chapter 32 – Prozac: It's what's for dinner.

After half a decade of resisting, I decided that maybe, just maybe, there was a chemical imbalance here. I decided to acknowledge that perhaps I needed to take something in order to reclaim my center.

My therapist was a psychologist. Since I did not believe in drug therapy, I never chose a psychiatrist. But now I saw that my therapy alone just was not working. I acknowledged the problem, and sought out help beyond my normal course of action. My psychologist agreed that was a good course of action.

I got a referral, and found a psychiatrist. I really didn't like the guy. My scheduled forty-five minute sessions with Dr. Patel were generally between ten and fifteen minutes. After long resistance, I gave in and let him prescribe an anti-depressant for me. Rather than give me a prescription with a refill for Prozac, he made me continue to return to him frequently in order to renew it.

It took a while, as such things do, to take effect. But in time, it began to work. Rather than my normal center feeling lonely and sad, I was finding myself content. And with that contentment, I was finding I was able to start working on my problems.

I was an even bigger mess than I thought. One emotion I had really not dealt with was my anger. Some fucker hit me with his car and left me for dead. The bastard didn't stop. He or she just drove on, as if nothing had happened. I could have been dead.

I lost a year of my life to my recovery. I spent months in a wheelchair, and months with a non-functional arm. I was completely reliant on others in order to go anywhere. I lost my independence. I was left with a deep, deep anger that I did not realize was eating at me, and it was manifesting itself in unusual ways: overeating, and bizarre sleep patterns. I didn't even realize that was what was causing it.

I can relate to The Incredible Hulk. Or rather, Mr. Banner, "Don't make me angry. You wouldn't like me when I was angry."

I had a nasty temper. Things got tossed. I killed more than one cordless phone when it impacted with a wall, or the floor. Other small things were often broken when I got angry. More than once I put a hole in a wall. Or a door. But I never hurt a living soul. My temper has always been reserved for the inanimate. I will not lash out at anyone, human or animal, with my anger. But walls are not so safe, and neither are phones.

There was a deep, deep sadness. Sadness for what I gave up when I chose Rachel over Tori. I had no idea what it was I had until I had given it up. It was not until that moment that I realized that I did, in fact, love Torrance. Too little, too late.

When I walked out her door, and chose Rachel instead, Tori closed her heart to me. She may have reopened it to allow the friendship back in, but we would never be lovers again. Another had her heart at this time, but I did not know that, and that is not my story to tell, it is Tori's.

So, not for the first time, and of course, not for the last time, I was at a crossroads in my life. I was recovered from my physical damage, but I was only just becoming aware of the depths of my psychological injuries. In some respects, healing the scars of emotional and psychological damage takes far more time and effort than healing from physical hurts. I had come a very long way. But I still had a long long way to go.

Therapy is a very useful tool. There are a lot of people out there who don't think so highly of therapy. I mean, c'mon kids, why not? It's not a bad thing to get in touch with one's emotional side. Life is never simple, is it?

Let me take a moment to tell all of you in the same boat that you are not alone. We are all in this fight together, and we have the right to be happy, and the black dog of depression is something many of us struggle with. I just felt the need to express that.

I needed to take steps to truly recover my independence. As such, I needed to find a job. The temp agency I had been using was running totally dry - nothing. They found me no work. That would not do. So I responded to various options, and another agency opted to take me on. They found me two opportunities, one that was not so good, and another that, while still not good, was less not good than the first. So, I went for the interview. My two interviewers, after only a few minutes with me, said pretty much the same thing.

"You do realize you are completely overqualified for this job?"

"Yeah, I know. But I gotta work somewhere."

Thus it was that I found myself employed again.

It was very very dull work. I mostly screened calls, and sent them to the appropriate tech people. In time, out of boredom, I created a tracking system. Then, when that ceased to keep me interested, I took it upon myself to learn the tech aspects of the equipment my group was supporting. Still, this was not exciting work. Not by any stretch of the imagination.

Meanwhile, back in the SCA, I was fencing again, twice a week. Both Johan and Maren were showing me new things along the way, and helping me to improve my game.

I am still loving this game, and my performance at the past champions in March really encouraged me. It's a pity I can't seem to repeat that combat competence. I think at least my overall fencing was showing an improvement.

My mental state was improving. The Prozac was certainly helping me find and maintain my center, which was a nice change. I was generally feeling less stressed about things. Relationships were really non-existent. Tori and I were just friends, though at times I very much longed to be more, but that was not to be. While I still occasionally saw Jill, we were far less involved, physically, than we used to be. Not to say we went completely without contact, but it was different.

Chapter 33 – Pornographic Pennsic.

Pennsic rolled around again, and this was a big one. Pennsic XXX. Yes, the "triple X" war. All kinds of amusing remarks were made with regards to that.

I opted again to camp down with my old group in the area called the Bog. I was growing more and more tired of the hike uphill every day to fence, and even with an armor dump atop the hill, in the camp of my local group, my relations there were getting more and more strained. Apart from Bob and one or two others, it was not what it used to be.

Again, I enjoyed the fencing, and watching the heavy combat, and as always the parties. This Pennsic, I was once again able to fight with my good right arm. It was nice to be, more-or-less, back to myself, if that would ever be the case again. Would I ever be "back to myself"? Or was "myself" fundamentally changed now? In what ways had the accident altered who I was? How had Warren Mushnik been changed? What had I learned about not only myself, but the world around me? I learned that I was stronger than a speeding car--well, at least in the end. At the point of impact, not so much. Car versus Warren, Car wins.

But when push came to shove, when I was faced with the choices of simply exist, die, or fight, I fought, and I gave it my all. I gave everything I had. I managed to beat the odds, recover better and faster than anyone had expected. I was whole again, for all intents and purposes, and lost really only a year to it all.

There was more. I learned who my friends were, and what that meant, and more, what they meant to me. I learned that my family loved me very much. I learned that I could, in fact, feel love. Maybe I didn't know it for what it was, and maybe I was a bit of a mess when it came to relationships, but I could feel love. Of course, it took some extreme bullshit to recognize it, and I almost lost the best friend I had ever had over it, but that was a part of this whole adventure.

So here I was once more, in the same place you can find me, pretty much, every August since 1996: camping with my rowdier friends, fencing with my usual companions, and enjoying a week of fun and sun, and such. Unlike last year, this year I wasn't napping every afternoon on the fencing field.

You know, they say that hindsight is twenty-twenty. So why am I finding, as I compose this, that mine seems to be nearsighted, much like my vision was before the Lasik? Or worse, farsighted. I can recall so well incidents from before that time, and speak much about many from after.

It has led me to see that I have lived, really, four lives. Well, far more than that, but it has greatly shaped who I am, as I write this memoir.

For the record, this particular style and genre is not my forte. I have been writing fantasies and fictions and sci-fi since I was a kid. Yes, I have kept a journal, from time to time, but to put my words to paper like this is an interesting and somewhat bizarre experience. At the same time, recounting such a life-changing experience has been rather cathartic.

Chapter 34 – The many lives of me.

Welcome to the many lives of me. You know, that could be the alternate title to this tome, as a whole. We begin in the Midwest, BD. FYI, BD means Before Divorce. My parents were together until I was five. We lived in Milwaukee, where my younger sister was born. Then my parents divorced.

Dad moved out East, and mom moved us to the Chicago 'burbs, to be nearer to her family. Thus began life, version one point oh, which I shall call AD, After Divorce.

When your parents' divorce and you are five years old, it tends to affect you on a deep, psychological level. It would be years of therapy for me before I fully coped with the divorce of my parents. I think, secretly, I blamed myself for the failure of their marriage. I was one of those oversensitive children. You know, the ones who fear adult things, like nuclear war and death and such, rather than the dark and boogiemen? Yeah, that was me as a kid. So I had a lot of issues. Then, to add to that fun, there was the divorce of my parents, with my dad choosing to move halfway across the country.

I found, as I got older, one of the ways I coped with things was to put on different facades. Each facade would be for a different group. Over the years, my groups shifted and changed, and so did the facade they saw from me.

My teachers saw one person, my family another, and my friends certainly more than one. Of course, I didn't realize what I was doing until much, much later in my life.

Growing up in the Midwest is very different than life on the East Coast. The Midwest is far more peaceful, far more calm, far less self-centered. The East is very much more paranoid, more in your face, more abrasive. In the Midwest, people are more apt to be courteous, because they are less concerned that someone is plotting behind their backs. Honestly, that's my experience with living in these two parts of the country.

After I graduated from high school, I opted to go to college "out east" anyhow. When I found myself living on the East Coast, my life changed rather drastically, as I learned more about myself and the people around me. First, let's talk about fitting in. I grew up surrounded by taller, blonder, non-Jewish people. I didn't quite fit in, to put it mildly, given that in high school I was generally from three to seven inches shorter than the other guys. On the East Coast, with a large Italian and Jewish population, I am average height. As such, I blend better out east.

Let's just clear something else up, okay? People have, on more than one occasion, attempted to 'out' me. It might be my love of show tunes, might be my ability to match colors, not just for myself, but for other people. It might be that at times I have been known to come across as somewhat flamboyant. For the record – as if several chapters along the way have not made this abundantly evident--I like women, too much, sometimes. Men, and the penis in particular, do nothing for me.

Having come from the Midwest, and it being the nineteen eighties and early nineties, the notion of a homosexual man was nothing but a vague concept I had heard tell of. No problem, it's a unique concept to me. Then I do my first tech crew in college theatre, and my tech director? Gay as the day is long - no question. He was a nice guy, and I was unconcerned by it.

There is a day, every year, called National Coming-Out Day. On that day a large number of homosexual men and women will declare their orientation, and throw off the shackles of the repression and oppression of the hetero world they are living in. There is an area of the main quad, on the Ithaca campus, called the Free Speech Rock. At that rock, annually, the local Bi, Gay, Trans and Lesbian support group holds a rally on National Coming-Out Day.

I encountered that rally first as a freshman. Not to be confused with those coming out, I gave it a wide, wide pass. Sophomore year, I did not go out of my way to avoid the Free Speech Rock on that day. Junior year, I was nearby, just observing the rally. Senior year, I was at the rally, supporting a friend who was coming out, along with the rest of my companions. It is amazing how our attitudes can evolve in just a few short years.

Anyhow, college was the beginning of life three: CL, or College Life, and after. It reshaped the way in which I approached much of my existence, and is probably familiar to many.

Then I got hit by a car.

Such a simple statement can have such a chilling effect, no? With that began the next stage of my life, PA, or Post Accident, and once more, the way in which I lived my life took a serious, fundamental shift. Why have I evolved, changed, then evolved again so many times? How come I can never seem to find one center, and stick to it? I learned, not so long ago, that one's center sometimes shifts. I realized that despite finding my center, for a while, it moved on me. So that gets added to the mix. What a mindfuck, huh?

After all the years I have spent in therapy, I seriously considered for a time going into psychology, or some form of therapy, for my own career. But as much as I love helping other people, and as much as I enjoy playing self-analyst, it just never felt like the right path for me.

Ok, let's carry on, shall we?

Chapter 35 – My family becomes more loco - I mean, local.

After Pennsic XXX, I prepared for Marnie's arrival. My little sister had decided to go to grad school in New York City, so she moved herself out to one of the little townlettes in Hudson County, New Jersey, and became a resident of the area. Thus, my sister would be local. I really thought that moving out here would do Marnie some good.

I have spent a lot of my life as Marnie's chauffeur, chaperone, and more. I am the older brother, and have always been protective of her. She has an ex-boyfriend that I still intend, if I ever see the bastard again, to punch his lights out. I can be a bit over-protective of her. We get along pretty well, given our age difference of five years. Sometimes I think she is a know-it-all bitch, but then, I don't doubt she feels much the same about me. Though as a man, truth is, I can't be a bitch. So Marnie will be local. It will be the first time in over twenty years that dad will have his children so close. I wonder how that makes him feel?

As the march of time, well, marches on, I begin to feel more and more distant with regards to the locals and the SCA group. What is it with them, anyhow? Tori and I are OK, so why are so many of them still having issues with regards to me? Rachel certainly moved on, even she and I are okay now. So what the fuck is with these people, anyhow? How come, and this continues to be an issue in my world, people are so quick to judge, but totally unwilling to ask for *my side* of a given story? Why am I always forced to defend myself, and never just asked where it is I stand, or how I have come to the place I am at? Why am I always the bad guy?

Seriously, it's an ongoing issue that, in certain circles, I have this mostly undue reputation. Yes, admittedly, I have cheated from time to time, and yes, I don't deny, I haven't always been as social and loving as I should be to some woman I am dating. But I am not abusive, I am not neglectful, and I am not a bad person. So why is it no one ever asks for my side of this shit?

Even with a growing distance from the one group, another group of friends, mostly fencers, were getting closer. Close enough, in fact, that I was planning already to camp with them at Pennsic XXXI, rather than back down in the Bog with my old house. I don't know if it was me growing tired of the very late night partying, or the hike up the fucking hill. Pennsic was a long way off. There would be much that would be happening with my life between here and there. Of course, along the way, I had some interesting, and fucking bizarre moments.

The two year anniversary of my accident came and went without incident. I not only did not get hit by another car, but I also managed to avoid being gobsmacked by another large breasted blonde. Both, good plans. I had considered, for fear of a bad incident, locking myself away during this period, so as to avoid tempting the fates. Thinking the better of it, though, I decided that, no, with my luck, if I lock myself up in my house, there will be a bad fire, and that would just suck, so, no.

While I am still a big fan of taking a chance and doing some neat things, there are a few I will now seriously avoid, like skydiving. I figure, if I was the powers-that-be, and I saw *me* skydiving, following all that I have been through, I'd be, like, "No, you fucking dolt; I don't think so," and then my chute wouldn't open. The reserve chute would. But I'd probably find it to be either an anchor, or an anvil. So, I'd hit the ground pretty hard. Of course, to add to the humor of it, I would survive it. I would break, more-or-less, every bone in my body, save my right leg and right clavicle, since they are made of stronger stuff, now.

That is why, to my mind, skydiving is right out. Same goes for bungee jumping.

Even as my relations with the overall local SCA group were getting more and more distant and strained, I was still singing with the small choir we had formed. I had been a part of that chorus from the beginning, and singing has been a big part of my life. I have always been pleased to have a strong, even partly trained, singing voice. So, the weekly choir thing still had appeal.

I think that too many months of near normalcy may have passed. That would probably be why I had to return to bizarro-world for a time.

Chapter 36 – On bubblegum machines and flashing lights - uh oh!

It was a normal Monday evening, and I was driving to practice. There's nothing out of the ordinary in that. I hit the point where one highway merged with another. As I reached that point, I saw the cop.

I might as well get this out there. I am not a fan of the cops. I recognize that in a society of law, we need a police force to enforce that law. But the trouble is, all too often those guys wind up simply being ego maniacal pricks, with a license to carry a gun. My father refers to the police thus: Armed and dangerous, treat with respect. I am right there with that.

I will not deny that I am a lead foot. I have a bad habit of driving too fast from point A to point B. I love the feel of speeds in excess of the limits on various highways. One of many things I like about Arizona is that, in large expanses of the desert, the speed limit is greater than seventy five. Woo hoo!

Fine, I am a notorious speeder. However, I do not bob and weave in, out, and through traffic, nor do I cut people off along the way. I just go fast. So, how come they always manage to stop me?

Ok, so I go past the cop, and he pulls out. Fuck. No lights and sirens yet, so I take my exit not long after these highways merge. I make a couple turns, and now he puts on the lights. Shit. Fine. Bastard pulls me over.

"Sir, can I see your license, registration, and insurance?"

"Yeah, okay."

I dig out the necessary paperwork, and pass it over.

"You should know that you hit that ramp at seventy, and you were moving from a highway with a speed limit of fifty five to another with sixty five, so either way you were moving a little fast."

"Oh. Okay."

He goes to his cruiser to do his thing. I saw at least one of the other members of the choir pass me. At least they know where I am, and can have a good laugh at my expense. This is taking forever. I mean, sheesh, my license is clean. Mr. Cop returns to my window.

"Mr. Mushnik, were you previously a resident of the state of New Jersey?"

"Yeah, like three or four years ago."

"Can I have your social security number?"

Ladies and gentlemen, boys and girls, an important lesson here. Take note. Never, ever, rattle off your social security number to a cop. Play dumb. Claim you don't have it memorized, and your card is not on you. Trust me on that. I made the mistake of giving him this stupid nine digit number. Damn my memory. He returned to his cruiser.

Waiting. Waiting. What the fuck is he doing back there?

Mr. Cop returns. "Mr. Mushnik, could you step out of the car, please?"

"O - kay."

So I do. Then, we walk around to the back, so I am not in the line of traffic. Thank you, officer.

"Sir, do you have two hundred and fifty dollars cash on you?"

"Ummmm, no. Why?"

"I am afraid I am going to have to place you under arrest."

"Excuse me?"

"Your license is suspended."

No, it's not. "No, my license is clean. I haven't had any violations in a long long time now."

"No, sir, your New Jersey license is suspended."

What the fuck?

"I am a resident of the state of New York. I surrendered my New Jersey license when I moved."

"I'm sorry sir, your license is suspended. And if you don't have the cash to post bail, I have to take you in."

"This is ridiculous. Why would I have that much cash on me? Look, just follow me to an ATM and I will get it for you."

"I'm sorry, sir, please turn around and put your hands behind your back."

"You've got to be kidding. This is insane, my record is clean."

"Sir, we can do this the hard way, or we can do this the easy way. Trust me, you will far prefer the easy way."

So I turn around, and the son of a bitch handcuffs me. All you people who do the whole BDSM thing, my opinion is that you're nuts. Handcuffs hurt.

So the fucker tosses me into the back of his police cruiser. And we are now waiting for the tow truck to come and take my car to be impounded. That is unacceptable.

Fortunately, my friends knew where I was, and were beginning to worry, so they came looking for me. Henry and his daughter arrived, and the cop explained to them why he was arresting me. He did permit me to pass them my keys, so they could take my car for me. Henry also told me he'd collect the bail money to get me out.

It was insane.

Let me provide you with the background on this tale. New Jersey has some of the most bizarre rules when it comes to automobiles. For example, you can take the driver's test in something like seven different languages. When I moved into New Jersey, back in 1996, I managed to get pulled over for speeding - twice - in New York State. New Jersey has reciprocal agreements with New York, so I might as well have gotten ticketed in the Garden State.

Even though I had previously been licensed, over the course of nine years, in two other states, New Jersey treated me as a new driver, licensed a sum total of less than a year. So I was given no choice, and forced to take a probational driver's class. Two hours of my life given, and in return, I get three points knocked off my license. Good. But here's the catch. Any moving violation in the next year will land me a thirty to ninety day suspension. I cannot be without my driver's license for thirty to ninety days. I mean, honestly, who can? And isn't that a bit harsh for speeding? I mean, driving under the influence, or causing an accident, or cutting people off, I'd understand. I am just a lead foot.

Of course, I couldn't just have the threat, so I made an illegal U-turn one day, and was busted for it. Terrific. I received notice that my license would be suspended in three weeks for ninety days. I was planning to move anyhow.

I found my current apartment in New York State, signed the lease, and went immediately to the Department of Motor Vehicles, and New York reissued me my license.

Hell, I even remember when I surrendered my New Jersey license there, they guy at the DMV said, "Welcome back to New York." So I beat the suspension.

Well, here it was, July of '98. Somewhere along about October, I received a letter from the good State of New Jersey, and they were demanding that I pay a one hundred dollar insurance surcharge. Yeah, right, I am a resident of New York. Why would I pay a surcharge amount to New Jersey? I disregarded that notice.

Thus here I was, today, being arrested for a license that did not exist, but that had been suspended due to non-payment of the insurance surcharge. How do you justify that bullshit?

So the cop, asshole extraordinaire that he is, runs me into the station. Once there, he has me remove my shoes, and all items from my pockets. He then proceeds to lock me into a cell. I shit you not. Oh, but he allowed me to take with me my mobile phone.

I called my dad.

"Hi, Dad...I'm in jail. No, seriously."

I called Tori.

"You are never going to believe where I am calling you from."

It was unbelievable. The cop, mind you, never read me my rights. He just cuffed me and tossed me in a cell. I think the fucking handcuffs left bruises on my wrists.

My friends had gotten the money, and bailed me out. The cop informed me that I needed to have my non-existent New Jersey license reinstated, or I could be arrested for driving in the state. In addition, I had a court date set. It was just unreal, and not getting any less surreal.

First, Henry takes me to an ATM, so I can repay him for the bail money. Then I go to choir. And I share my tale of woe with all. I can't make this shit up. This is not fiction. Who needs fiction when shit like this happens? So now I cannot legally drive in New Jersey. And I really don't want to be arrested. Thus Bob and Henry run me to the New York state line, where I get in my car and drive home.

The next day, my dad took me to a DMV in New Jersey, so I could reinstate my non-existent license. This issue would not resolve quickly. I had to go to court - thrice.

Now, in most states, or at least New York, when you have a traffic violation, you go to court. You see the judge. You plead not guilty, you then speak to the officer who gave you the ticket. Then you work out a deal.

Once, in upstate New York, I did that. The cop was a nearly retirement-aged State Trooper, and he had come into court at the end of his day off. We had a lovely conversation about his new chipper/shredder he'd spent the day playing with. In the end, he let me plea to a far lesser violation. Of course the fine, including the court fee, was a bit stiff, but better than the points and the rise in my insurance premium.

That is not how it works in New Jersey. In Jersey, you go to court. The judge talks at you for a few moments, and then you stand in line to see the local town prosecutor. You aren't just there with traffic violators. Actual, honest-to-god, shackled prisoners who have committed real crimes are also in court with you.

I go and wait to speak to the prosecutor. He is exactly the stereotype that I expect. Nice suit, slicked back hair, sharp as a tack and dull as fuck - a power-obsessed jerk.

"Well sir, you don't have a lot of options," he tells me. "You might want to get an abatement, delay your case, and speak to a lawyer." Okay. So I do that. Now I get to come back to court next month.

I decide to consult the lawyer who had previously gotten me money out of my insurance company following my accident. He gave me some advice on how to handle the prosecutor. Round two: I am now informed that that advice will not serve me, and that I may be subject to an additional suspension of my non-existent New Jersey license. Oh, and, just for shits and giggles, for violating the insurance surcharge rules, the judge may opt to fine me three thousand dollars. What the fuck?

Now I seek out a better lawyer. Round three: The lawyer speaks to the prosecutor. I don't do anything but sit in the courtroom and watch the judge power-trip. My lawyer returns.

"It's all set. You're free to go, there will be no fines. You just gotta pay the court fees, and since this is New Jersey, it won't affect your insurance."

You're kidding, right?

So, I get back some of my bail money, the rest pays off my court fees, and it is over.

Kind of.

Reinstating a license that had been surrendered to another state: one hundred and fifty dollars. Paying a lawyer to clear up the bullshit with the state of New Jersey: six hundred dollars. Court fees: eighty dollars. Receiving notice of an Insurance surcharge at the end of the year: priceless.

I kid you not. I received another insurance surcharge from the state of New Jersey. One hundred dollars. And, that would be recurring for the next three years. Suffice it to say, albeit grumpily, I paid it. It never ceases to amaze me what red tape one must cut because of bureaucracy.

Chapter 37 – Why do I keep swimming in the dating pool?

I was still working at the same job, but remained a temp. In fact, they kept me as a temp for a long, long time, something like seventeen months. I tried to find another job, but there were no other jobs to be had. The market was beginning to suck, and then the American public, no, sorry, the bullshit Electoral College, elected a moron to the White House, and matters got worse. But there have already been volumes written about that. And surely more to come. So let's just leave my political commentary here. This is a more personal story about a fairly normal man.

Well, in some respects normal. Not that I would ever consider myself normal, per se. I am not. Quirky in some ways, bizarre in others, a bit odd from time to time, and, in some respects, perfectly normal. I sleep, I eat, shower, shave, shit, daydream, work, and do all the same things everyone else does. Celebrities are rare. We common folk are, well, common.

Anyhow, I had to earn money to pay the rent and other bills. Plus having a social life can be pretty cool. Some might consider that a luxury, but I think of it as more of a necessity.

Two nights a week fencing, and choir every other Monday, though that was starting to wear thin along with most every other aspect of my local SCA group. I had long ago been forgiven by Tori. Why in the hell were they still holding on? Of course, my next couple of dating choices may have had something to do with it.

First there was Regina. For the first time in a long time, she was older than me. In fact, she had a good six or seven years on me. She was completely my type, and a very talented, intelligent woman.

We started off just hanging out. I don't entirely remember how we met. Well hanging out led to making out which led to sex. And that was good. Really good, actually. Sex with Regina was a lot of fun. But Regina herself was, uh, eccentric. I would even hazard to say she was a bit on the nutty side. I think her mind occasionally wandered to places in great detail. Places where only her mind seemed to visit, you see.

At first I ignored this. But over time, it was a deal breaker, as they call them. She was just too crazy for me to be serious about. You know what they say, never date anyone crazier than yourself.

Then there was Daria. We began as just friends, nothing more. We started to hang out from time to time, though with no intent beyond a pair of friends spending some time together. Well as things sometimes do, it turned one night. And before I knew it, we got to the sex. I will state, for the record, that in my opinion, there is nothing wrong with casual sex. It is a natural act that we desire to partake of. Religion and other institutions insist that sex is dirty and strictly meant for procreation. To them I say, how do you know that? If that is the case, how come sex feels so damned good?

Seriously, if sex was meant strictly for procreation, don't you think it would be far more utilitarian? I mean, like when a couple were both primed to mate, their foreheads would glow pink or some such? Nothing of the sort, sex for procreation is, in fact, a crap shoot. You might impregnate your partner, or you might not. But either way, if you both chose to go there, you will both experience the pleasure of sex. Because sex is taboo in this country, in a lot of respects, we have turned it into something it really isn't. America attempts to hold to these asinine puritanical values that were, more-or-less, outmoded moments after they were conceived, yet all advertising sells sex. Buy that car, wear that sweater, drink that soda, and you will get laid! Talk about your schizophrenic mixed signals!

Let me set the record straight right here. I sent no one any mixed signals. Daria and I never discussed exclusivity. And while Regina and I did, we mutually decided against it. There were no rings, promises, or other ideas put out there with regards to these relationships, for what they were. No one was boyfriend or girlfriend, we would hang out and do things, frequently naked.

Regina and Daria overlapped some. Certainly not in the sense of me going off from sex with the one to sex with the other in the same night or anything like that, but more in the sense that I was with one on a night, and the other on a different night. And I didn't think I was doing anything that could mislead either woman to think we had anything more than a fun, casual relationship.

Did I mention that Regina was a little crazy? Yeah, well, fast forward to an SCA event, of all things, and Daria and Regina getting drunk together at a campfire, then talking about men, and sex, and…hey, wait a minute, what do you mean we've been sleeping with the same man?

I accept the argument that, hey, you know, maybe I should have told them both about the other. But, again, I counter that both knew there was no exclusivity here. So my only mistake was in not detailing with whom I might be with during our non-exclusive relationships.

Well suddenly I am in the doghouse, and, in an unexpected twist, Regina claims we were dating exclusively, and I have cheated on her. Wait a minute, hold the phone! We dated exclusively about a week before we mutually concluded that it was not what either of us wanted. And it was long before this incident occurred. Somehow the whole thing degenerates into a Warren-bashing experience. Out of nowhere other women in the local group whom I have had relations with in the past are popping out of the woodwork, and debating if they, too, are involved in this overlap. Then the rumors began.

"Did you hear that Warren/William was sleeping with like five different women at the same time?"

"Oh, oh, hey, did you here that William is fucking like seven women?"

"I heard that Warren was tent hopping at some event, and slept with, like, three or four women, in the same night!"

"Did you know that when William was the one who welcomed all the newcomers to the group, he was using his position to pick up and sleep with women?"

Wait, wait, stop the story! I have a question…when all this was going on, and I was fucking all these women, where the hell was I? How come I missed out on all this fun?!

A valuable lesson, however, was learned by me on that one. Don't fight a rumor. If someone comes to you and questions the rumor, and wants your side of the story, give it to them, but don't just volunteer your side. If you do that, either no one will care, or they will disbelieve, and think you are defending yourself because some part, or all of, the rumor is true. Years later, the fallout from this bullshit has yet to fully evaporate.

Suffice it to say, it was this incident that drove the final nails into the coffin of the local group, with regards to my relationship to it. I walked away from the local SCA group when it became abundantly clear that my service was neither wanted nor appreciated any longer, and that my person was not of the sort that they wanted around. I would really have appreciated if at least one of the people, whom I used to call friend, had actually asked for my opinion, my side of the matter, rather than assuming the worst and further turning on me. But that did not happen.

That was my social life over the next couple of years after my accident. Amazing, in hindsight, how of those who were so close, so attentive during the time I was injured, so few are still close. And I cannot fully blame their personalities for this, mine is certainly not what it was at the start of this episode of my life. Warren Mushnik pre-accident was a very different man from the one post-accident. Post-accident Warren was a bit more blunt, a bit more liable to take a chance on something because he was much more acutely aware of how precious, and how incredibly fragile the human body can be.

Chapter 38 – Working for the man.

The job front did not improve. Sure, I basically created the templates for all aspects of my job, and wrote my own description of duties, but still remained a temp - forever, it seemed. It lasted seventeen months. I tried to find another job. I looked around everywhere I could think of for a better job. Again, the near-perfect vision that hindsight offers, I really wish I had made a better choice of major in college.

So dear reader, if you happen to be a college student, and you have a major but no goal, or a direction without goal, or no major yet, choose wisely. Don't just choose for the sake of making a choice, make sure you can do something with your degree. Sure, you need at least a Master's degree nowadays to do anything that really uses your college education, but trust me on this one, if you don't choose something that can give you direction and focus, you might just find yourself, when school is over, standing at a crossroads, with no clear path before you. The road less traveled is a worthwhile endeavor, but make sure you take plenty of water along, plus trail mix, and pee before you start traveling. Food and rest stops are not always readily available along that road.

At long last, the structure of the company was changed, and I was hired on, complete with benefits and an actual job title. Did I get any credit for creating the operational procedures for that job? Of course not, that would imply I was more than just a cog in the great corporate engine. I found almost no satisfaction in being a real employee of the company. My job actually got worse, as the corporate structure for the computer tracking system we were forced to use was outmoded back in the early 1990's, and this was, like, 2002. I understand budgetary constraints, but you have got to be realistic about some of these things. Like, without an up-to-date infrastructure, you are dooming yourself to obsolescence. Trust me on this one.

I certainly do not claim to know how best to run a business. If I did, I think I'd probably be running one by now. But I have seen, on both the small and grand scale, precisely how *not* to run a business. Believe me, sometimes knowing how not to do something is far more powerful than possessing the know-how. I have watched how to fail on different scales. It simply does not cease to amaze me how similar mistakes can have very different effects on different sized corporate entities.

I have also learned that corporate America and I are a match made in divorce court. I am too rebellious, too independent, and too much of a free thinker to properly fit into any company's mold. I have tried again and again to get into that world, so that I might pay my bills and have a life. I could go off on a total digression about my relationship with money, but that is not relevant at this juncture. It should be noted, with proper irony, that while I managed to work as a temp for this monster company for seventeen months, I only lasted six months as a legitimate employee.

Technically, I guess I was fired. But I defy you to find the manager who did it, he was laid off not long after me. I think I pissed off the big boss. He told us that, if we had suggestions for means to improve the company, and how we conducted business, we needed to share those. We needed to make him aware, so that he could help us make them happen, and help us help our clients to work more intelligently. Bullshit.

The lesson I learned here is, in regards to a big corporate infrastructure such as I was working with, never volunteer information of that kind. They only say that to make you feel empowered, they actually don't want to empower you. I suspect that might be because you might show them up, or something. I am not being egotistical. I am calling it exactly as I see it.

I went ahead and made some suggestions to improve how we did our job. Then, suddenly, out of the blue, they completely surprise me. I am warned that it is imperative that I be at my desk at spot-on nine am. In fact, it would be best were I a bit early. The work day starts at nine. That has never been an issue before. Where is that coming from? Would anyone reasonable consider nine-oh-two late? I mean, given variances in watch settings, and a desk-job where you are never seen, and only heard over-the-phone kind of job? We're making something of a whopping two minutes? Well it was significant enough, apparently, for me to be formally written up.

I had been a minute or two late before. So had most of my other coworkers. What's up with that? Then it happened a second time. More legitimately, there came a day when I was, in point of fact, ten minutes late. Never mind that it had been pouring rain that day, and everyone in the office was ten to thirty minutes late, and I do mean everyone. There was a major accident at the entrance to the parking lot. And yet, for that reason, they fired me.

Or maybe, as I postulated at that time, it was actually because I would have figured out what they were setting up, and recognized that it would have made the work that I, and my co-workers, all of whom were hired at the same time, did obsolete. They fired me before they could start the layoffs. I found out that those, in fact, began less than a month after I was let go. I know it's a lie to tell interviewers that I was laid off from that job, but could they ever find any of the people involved to prove otherwise? To all intents and purposes, is that really any different?

Now I have managed to get ahead of myself. In a couple of chapters I'm going to mention that I am still at this job, and you're going to be all, like, wait, I thought you got fired? And I'm, like, well, yeah, I told you about that, but I got ahead of myself, and it won't happen until a little way further ahead. Sorry for the confusion in said forthcoming chapter.

Chapter 39 – Round and round it goes, where it stops, nobody knows?

A year and a few months after the physical damage, the emotional and psychological damage popped up. After a lot of soul searching, and a bit of denial, I gave in to the fact that I had a chemical imbalance, and I found a psychiatrist and began a prescription of Prozac. I had very much resisted doing that. I really did not want to be on that drug, or any such drug, for that matter. I wanted to use meditation or exercise or something else to get ahold of my emotional state.

Once the drug got into my system, I began to get clear. I was able to reach and maintain a place of being centered, of being calm, of being at piece. I was no longer sad, or depressed, or always lonely. I just was. I would daresay I was content.

Contentedness is something I think we often overlook. We try so hard to be happy, and use so many artifices to get there. I think if we simply strove to be content, for the most part, all the rest would fall into place, and happiness, true happiness, would come more easily.

The drug helped me to be content, and it was certainly a better feeling than the sadness or loneliness I had grown too readily accustomed to.

Warning – incoming rant! Women and children to the lifeboats!

The problem in this nation, with drug therapy, is that people use it like some sort of quick fix. While I know a lot of people, including myself, for whom Prozac and Paxil and Welbutrin, and all have done good work, people seem to not understand a fundamental tenet of how, exactly, these drugs are meant to be applied: in concert with therapy. The drugs alone do you only limited good, because while they might work to make the serotonin flow better, without the therapy to address the issues in the first place, you only really get about halfway there. I know multiple people who have been put on the drugs, but who never received any real treatment, per se. To be fair, I see you are doing something to help yourself, but is it enough? Are you actually addressing the problem, or using the drugs to avoid it?

Seriously, that's a big deal. A lot of people don't comprehend that a large part of what makes these drugs so useful is that they help to make the therapy actually effective.

Then there is another minor issue. Some people have no problem popping pills. There are pills that will fix nearly everything, and new ones coming out all the time to make us better, stronger, faster, wiser, etc. So for those people, the notion of adding another chalky consumable to their system is no big deal. I am not one of those people. As shown with regards to the powerful painkillers I was on after my accident, I would prefer an approach using less rather than more. I only take a painkiller when the pain interferes with my life. I take a decongestant when my nose is too plugged up to breathe through. I really use all drugs as a last resort. Prozac was like that too. I had intended to only give it six months, but was still working things out once that time came and went. So I extended that period instead to a full year. I am pretty sure Doctor Patel didn't see this one coming.

"So you are doing well, and feeling better?"

"Yes. So take me off this stuff."

"How's that?"

"I want to get off the Prozac now."

"But it's working so well."

"Exactly. It's done its job. So I want to get off it."

Prozac and its brethren are not meant to be taken forever, at least not for most. They are meant to be a stop-gap, they are designed to be a temporary assistant. In time, one is supposed to be able to go off them.

I had seen it before in others, and like any good drug, Prozac withdrawal is ugly. Depression, anger, overeating, sleep patterns even more fucked up then normal. But soon I was through with that, and I was back to that contentment, without the drug.

I was also done with Dr. Patel. That was good too. Apart from providing me with the prescription for the anti-depressant, he didn't do much for me.

Let me just state, for the record, that depression is a pretty serious problem. We do not show it the proper respect we should, and we do not treat it like the disease it is. There is no shame in suffering from depression. The shame is that too many people still see it as a weakness. As such, too many people feel ashamed about admitting to it. There is no shame in depression. Don't let anyone tell you otherwise.

That said, it should also be stated that there is no shame in getting treatment for depression. Self-care is of vital importance, and if you are coping with depression getting treatment is invaluable. You are too important not to be cared for. Just wanted you to know that.

Chapter 40 – A milestone. Please tell me there aren't any pictures?

My thirtieth birthday rolled up on me. It was hard to believe that I was turning thirty. I had come so close to not getting past twenty seven. Nearly three years had passed since my accident. Life was returning to normal-ish. At least as normal as my life ever is.

Little did I know, my father and sister plotted a surprise party for me. They got Tori to conspire, and give them a list of my friends, so they could contact them. They then rented a private room at an excellent middle-eastern restaurant my family had grown fond of.

So that they could all prepare and get there ahead of me, I had to pick up Marnie's boyfriend, Leroy. Leroy is a decent guy, but not by any stretch of the imagination what my mother would wish for Marnie. My mom really would like for Marnie and I to marry Jews. Leroy is not Jewish. Neither is his skin white. You can imagine what that did to my mom's psyche.

I waited for Leroy, getting anxious because he was taking his sweet time. I mean, what was he doing? Why wasn't he ready? After what felt like an eternity, finally, he showed up. We went to the restaurant.

Dad and Marnie and Lucy were waiting for me.

"Ah, good, you are here," the owner said. "I wanted to wait to show off our newly remodeled space to you all, and now I can."

In we went, and when the doors opened, there were a huge group of my friends.

"Surprise!"

I actually like surprises. As such, that was so cool!

I sat near one end of the table, ironically enough both Rachel and Tori were near. Yes, Rachel and Tori had become friendly in the intervening time, and were both at my thirtieth birthday party. Amazing how different all out lives were now, and that we could all sit at a table for dinner together.

My mom had of course wanted to be here, but getting in from Chicago would not have worked for her. So she sent me a little gift. A little gift that provided me with years of embarrassment my friends would not soon let go of.

Mom sent a Gorilla-gram. No, I am not making this up. A man in a safari hat, and his partner in a Gorilla suit. It was a big to-do, and the Gorilla suited partner - well, she danced for me, and gave me a lei, and pictures were taken, and hilarity ensued.

Incidentally, years later, I received, as a holiday present from Porsche a flying, humping monkey. Yes, my friends have very twisted senses of humor.

I thought at first the gorilla-suited woman might be my mom, but, thank the powers-that-be, she wasn't. Leave it to my mom's, um, different sense of humor to pull something like that.

A slight digression here, but it's taken a long time for my mother to reconcile her tastes versus my tastes. They are very, very different. As mentioned before, I have two very different families represented by my mom and stepdad, versus my dad and stepmom. How different? Let me put it to you this way: my dad and stepmom are into wine and cheese, drive luxury cars, and listen to NPR. My mom and stepdad, on the other hand, are into girly fruity drinks and popcorn, drive a minivan, and listen to oldies. Get the picture?

At any rate, I faced thirty with some trepidation. I had thought my life would be in a very different place by the time I got there. Yes, much had happened along the way, but still, that what not where I'd thought to be. So now what?

For a whole host of reasons, my thirtieth year was a rough one. There were several high points, but the trouble was, I attached an awful lot of stigma to the number thirty. I am sure I would have been better off had I not done so. Once more I look to hindsight, and see it with a twenty/twenty clarity that it would be really nice to see the present and future in, sometimes. I wonder if someone will every invent something like that.

Chapter 41 – The adventure continues. Go west, young man!

After my thirtieth birthday, in the fall of 2002, I had an opportunity to travel to Arizona. I had been there numerous times over the years, as my grandparents on my father's side had retired there. There is a certain beauty and warmth to the desert that I find both comforting and pleasant.

The reason to make this trip was an annual SCA event called the Known World Academy of the Rapier, shortened usually to KWAR. That event would draw teachers and fencers from around the nation to share ideas, and techniques, and to fight people you just don't get a chance to play with often. I had to go. Also, this would be my first opportunity to visit my paternal grandmother for the first time in something like five or six years, maybe longer.

I hate flying, it should be noted. Not out of fear, just discomfort. Airplanes are not designed with seats that are going to be tremendously comfortable for any two-to-three people in a row who have shoulders beyond forty inches wide, and a waist of greater than thirty four inches or so. Seriously. If you take a standard row of any airplane passenger cabin, and you sit three men with a waist of greater than thirty eight inches and shoulders beyond forty six, there's going to be a lot of scrambling for armrests. I always seem to manage to find the really turbulent flights, too.

Part of my new status as a full-time employee of the corporation had been paid vacation time. It happened that I had more coming to me than I would use by year's end, and it was use-it-or-lose it. So I packed up my fencing gear in a hard shell golf tube, checked my bags, and flew to Phoenix. There is just something about Arizona that always feels like home to me. Don't know what it is.

Of course, I was not the only attendee from out here on the East that went. Several others, including Jon, who was serving as Society marshal at the time, were going as well. KWAR is like a convention, including a hotel where we usurp the various conference rooms and halls for our purposes. Only with a lot more swords and armor than an average board meeting.

I wonder what a corporate board meeting would be like if they had fencing weapons involved?

I had a blast at that event. I saw some folks I only ever see at Pennsic. One friend, Cameron, I came across retelling a story that, incidentally involved me. I was just outside the circle, and my back was to him, as he told the story. Now picture this a moment: Cameron stands about six foot four, and is thin as a rail. Remember that I am five foot six and chunky; that is important to the story. Oh, and imagine this story being told in a thick English accent. Not an affectation, Cameron is originally from the Old Country.

"So we're guarding the entrance, William and I," Cameron is narrating, "And this poor bastard, paying no attention at all, just passes right before us, ignoring us entirely. Simultaneously, like we'd planned it, we both place a blade on his opposite shoulder, wind up crossing in front of his throat, and in sync state 'My lord, you are dead.' The Marshal atop the nearest hay bale could not stop laughing."

Since we do not desire to actually hurt our friends, in order to allow a more realistic melee situation, we have a method for committing a 'kill' from behind. Rather than stab someone in the back, you place your blade upon their shoulder, and give them a short, courteous phrase such as the aforementioned, "My lord, you are dead." I have also heard, "You have been killed from behind," and, perhaps less courteously but more amusingly, "Who's your daddy?"

That had been the coolest kill from behind I had ever taken part of. Death from behind and above as Cameron dropped his blade on the poor bastard's shoulder, Death from behind and below as I reached up and did the same. Hilarity. I wonder if that story is only funny if you know the game, or happened to be there at the time?

"That was pretty cool, wasn't it?" I interjected at that point. Cameron whirled around, and wrapped me in a bear hug.

"And this, my fine audience, is William himself. True story."

"Yup, true story," I agreed, and we laughed.

When you see me standing beside Cameron, and can observe for yourself the disparity in height and proportions, it just adds to the silliness of the tale.

I got to fight with a lot of folks I don't normally cross blades with, made some new friends, and all around had a fantastic time.

I also got to go visit my grandmother. I have been very fortunate in this life not only to have known both of my parent's mothers, but also my grandfather on my dad's side, and two great-grandmother's on his side as well. An upside to having young parents, I suppose. My grandpa Warren died when my mother was a child, and it is he whom I was named for. My mother's mom, Grandma Bessy, was admittedly my favorite. She was there for me a lot while I was growing up, was really good to both me and Marnie, and she was the sweetest woman. She was always getting up early, going for walks, and lived on her own as long as I knew her. I was deeply saddened by Grandma Bessy's passing. May she rest in peace.

My only remaining grandparent was my Grandma Enid. When my grandpa Stan passed away back in 1990, Grandma Enid began her decline. First her body, and then slowly her mind would follow. Grandpa Stan was her anchor to this world. This was the first time I would see her in a long, long time. Her mind was still decent enough, but she could barely walk. I visited the home she and Grandpa Stan had built in Scottsdale, stirring a lot of old memories.

Grandma Enid was always an eccentric. Also, she was a bit of a snob. And she had her ways. There were certain things that were verboten in her presence. She was very quirky with regards to them. For example, no bouncing on your bed. Never mind that she would sit on the edge of her bed and bounce some. No chewing on your ice, as she herself chewed on ice, and, for real, don't stick your elbows on the table.

That one was driven home one Thanksgiving when I was a teen. I made the mistake of taking the seat next to her, and my elbows rested upon the table. She made her distaste of this practice know, as she stuck a fork in my elbow. I am not making this up. She poked my elbow with her fork to get me to take it off the table. While that did not stop me from putting my elbows on the dinner table, it did keep me from sitting at the place beside her ever again.

The other thing of note, with regards to Grandma Enid, is that she loved to play favorites. That did not hurt me, largely because, for over twenty years, I was the last male in my family line. My aunt and uncle had produced three daughters before they managed to get a son. That did, however, hurt Marnie.

My father was not Grandma Enid's favorite, my uncle was. As such, Uncle Jim and his daughters got the better treatment. Marnie sort of got a lot of cold shoulder from Grandma. Let's not even get into her opinion towards my mother. That was a love/hate, well, honestly, mostly mutual dislike, relationship.

I went and saw my grandma, and it was good to see her. She was clearly, genuinely grateful that I visited her.

Grandma had a twenty-four hour nursing service caring for her, helping her walk, which she did not do so much, and preparing food or picking it up or taking her out for meals. Again, this was not actually boding well for her overall health, but that is a whole other story.

It was, apart from a couple trips to Chicago for family obligations, my first real trip since my accident. As November thirtieth approached again, it passed without incident, marking the third year since my accident.

Chapter 42 – The Adventure Continues, Part 2. Life, the Universe, and Everything.

Three years have passed since I was hit by a car while crossing a street. I walk without a limp. I can fence. I have regained over ninety percent of the usage of my right arm, and while the titanium plates pull my shoulder forward sometimes, there have been few long lasting ill effects.

I was working on the sequel to my first fantasy novel during slow periods at work, and on my off time as well. It is my intent to make that series four books, plus prequels. I intend to publish them someday. I have been trying for a number of years to get an agent to represent me, and while I had brief representation, I had to end that association because he proved to be less than useful for my purposes. Fantasy was just not his genre.

Meanwhile, following the tragedy of 9/11, Tori had chosen to take a new and risky path.

Not long after we first met, Torrance shared with me her dream. And that dream was to open a holistic store. I had even, on a trek to Chicago before my accident, plotted with her some ideas for the store.

The terror attacks had changed her. Tori didn't just read about them in the paper or watch the horror of the towers falling on TV. She witnessed it with her own two eyes from her office on the Hudson River, on the New Jersey side. She watched the second plane hit the tower. She watched the first tower fall before she chose to leave. I met her a few hours after it all went down, and en route to her house, saw for myself the monstrous smoke cloud where the towers once stood.

Despite working for a CCTV security company, we had no functional televisions at my office. The internet connection we had was slow, so streaming video was not doable, and not terribly available in 2001. We knew something happened, we knew it was an act of terrorism before it was decided we could leave work for the day. Additionally, as one coworker pointed out, we were working out of the tallest building in Rockland County. What if there were more plains aiming for tall targets out there?

Tori and I went to her parent's place in the far northwest corner of New Jersey, away from New York, in case something further happened. I saw for the first time on TV what she had seen with her own eyes. But the disaster set her resolution to take control of her destiny, and to begin her own business.

Tori took a class on how to be an entrepreneur, and began to scout locations.   After a year or so, she found the perfect place. The building was being totally stripped to its studs, and renovated. Tori would have the opportunity to build her store from the ground up. She could have her space precisely how she wanted it. Thus it began, and we gathered to work on building her dream.

It had evolved beyond just a holistic gift store; it had become a two room spa as well.   In addition to that, Torrance partnered with her younger sister to make it all happen. The first time we all gathered in that space, it was nothing but concrete and wall framing. We were assembling custom built bases for the shelves.

There was a certain serendipity to the timing of all of it. I lost my job in January 2003, or so, and that provided me with the time to help Tori, her sister, father, and various other volunteers, with the work to make the space her own. Even though I was looking for work, and collecting unemployment, I was spending a great deal of my time at the site, helping to build furniture, paint walls, hang lighting, and do all the other crazy stuff that contractors would often do, but we were doing it ourselves. There was a certain satisfaction in working like that.

In February, I again traveled to Arizona. This time, Tori came along. But we had different destinations. She was going north to Sedona, for a spiritual retreat, a pre-store opening escape to give her focus. I was going to an SCA event near Phoenix.

Estrella War draws nearly eight thousand people. It's much like Pennsic, only smaller. I had, through my household, made contacts who gave me a space to camp. Cameron, living only hours away by car, in New Mexico, provided me with a tent.

I was the lone representative of the Eastern Rapier Army. The marshal in charge of fencing at the event loved playing that off.

"The side that has the fewest combatants will get the entire Eastern Rapier Army - William!" Yup. An army of one.

Damn did I have fun, though. I fought til my heart's content. I ran with an excellent army from the Kingdom or Artemesia, which for those of you not in the SCA, is Utah, Idaho, and some other spaces in that general vicinity.

I also happened to be the only guard of the Queen of the East present at Estrella, so I spent some of my time off the fields escorting her. She, fortunately, was a lot of fun, so that was not an unpleasant duty.

It amazed me that, in many respects, these foreign fencers gave me a lot more respect than my own peers. Of course, I probably fought better overall because I felt far less pressure to perform.

After Estrella, I traveled to Sedona to meet Tori. We shared a hotel, and a rental car. She had one more day of her retreat, and I had heard amazing things about the red rock vistas of Sedona. I took her to her retreat, and randomly chose a spot to go hiking.

I may be a heavy man, and always overweight, but I love hiking. I have since I was a teen, and going to overnight camp. Sedona has some amazing places to hike. On this trip, I discovered Boynton Canyon. I hiked up and through the incredible red rocks, and while I did not recognize it for what it was at the time, I felt the incredible energy of the Earth herself in the famous vortices.

Ah, another connection to Reiki and my hooky-spooky side, but yes, I could feel the incredible energy in this place. As I found an absolutely astounding vista to pause and journal in, a sense of peace like nothing I had ever experienced before overtook me. The energy, the warmth, and the beauty of Sedona were like nothing I had ever felt before. I found a level of inner peace even greater than while I'd been on the Prozac.

I was looking out upon the most picturesque, gorgeous landscape I had ever seen. It was like something out of a dream, the reds and oranges and browns of the stone, the few sparse bushes and cacti, and the sun playing upon the rocks, creating shadows that had a life all their own.

It was as if someone had hit my reset button. I felt rejuvenated, overjoyed, and simply thrilled to feel it. Nothing I had ever seen before could have prepared me for the beauty of that place. I would return to Sedona again. I have hiked at numerous other points and experienced other vortices in that place. I look forward to returning whenever I can. Who would have thought, just over three years ago, not only would I walk again, but I would be hiking about rocky hills in Arizona?

The flight home was uneventful, save the awful movie that was playing. I won't name it, and it's not like I had anywhere else to be on that flight. But I still want those ninety minutes of my life back!

When I got home, there were a number of things that seemed different in my life. I was content to be writing, and working with Tori and her family to make the store happen. I was not seeing anyone, which was probably a good thing. It is a lesson, in fact, I really need to spend more time with. I am not very good with relationships. I mention this a lot because I think I need to bear it in mind more often than I do.

I suck at dating, yet I am not so fond of being single. None-the-less, it is important to note that much of the dating badness I take the blame for is not entirely my fault. I am not trying to throw the blame to my exes, mind you. I am just pointing out that not only does it take two to Tango, it also takes two to completely fuck up a relationship. Of course, when the whole Rachel thing went down, and Tori was feeling so devastated, she made a point of badmouthing me. That made her feel better, and if it destroyed my reputation along the way, hey, I fucking deserved it. I think that may have been a bit harsh, but that was where her mind was going.

I have had only a few longer, more serious relationships, and several shorter but intense ones, and then a few others. That doesn't even begin to cover fuck buddies and the like.

One of the reasons I am so bad at relationships is fear. I watched my parents relationship disintegrate, in my childhood, and it left me very fearful of repeating the process. I did not want to get involved with someone, go through all the stuff like living together and engagement and marriage, only to produce children and then divorce and fuck them up much like I had been.

Really positive attitude there, huh? So yeah, relationships are surely not my forte.

Chapter 43 – The Adventure Continues, Part 3. Karma, and moving the floor.

I spent the rest of 2003 working on my writing craft, and helping Tori and her family put her store together. I was a big part of that operation, doing painting, carpentry, and whatever else was needed. We were building a space that would be unique and pleasant and a real respite for those visiting it. I was proud to be a part of it.

Tori's plans for her store were ambitious. She and her sister had no experience with the spa world at all, but she pushed forward, and we were creating a unique, beautiful space. It was going to be impressive. Unique colors, rounded corners, lights and river stones and oxidized copper accents. It was hard to believe that over ninety percent of the furnishings came from IKEA.

IKEA furniture comes in one of two forms; damned simple to construct, and what-rocket-scientist-dreamt-this-nightmare up? One piece in particular, called by the Swedes, Akarum, came to be known as the Arkham Asylum, after the lock-up for criminals from the Batman comics. They drove us builders nearly that crazy along the way.

Details meant a lot. We painted everything. And I mean everything. Take, for example, the vents. The air vents, for the heating a cooling system, were way up at the top of the walls. That put them at about fifteen feet or so. Well these vents, like most industrial products of that nature, were white. The walls around them were deep, chocolate brown.

So, I climbed a ladder, and removed the vents. I laid them out, then spray painted them a similar chocolate brown. Note the word similar. Anyone who can see color could tell they were not the same once they were back up on the top of the walls, so I chose to correct that. Tori's perfectionism can be contagious. I climbed the ladder again, with a paint brush, and the same chocolate brown that had been applied to the upper walls and the ceiling. I made a point of coating the grills for the vents, so that they blended in. When you go into the store, and look up, they disappear into the walls, as they should.

Damn, did a lot of effort go into making that place. I think that the love and caring we put into every aspect of its construction really made the energy of the space that much better. We had created a place of positive, healing comfort. To do that with a retail store is a real trick, and damned impressive. Tori and her sister and father are brilliant designers.

I also figured this was building me some additional, much needed positive karma. I had done enough along the way to take on negative karma, I think anything that turned that around was a good thing.

Was my accident karma? I don't know. Maybe. It's possible that I kind of asked for something like that to happen. I believe that consciousness does, in fact, create reality. As such, I want to be careful what I wish for, in case I get it. Yet at the same time, I hope for great things in life. I want to publish my stories, and share my visions, worlds, and characters with others. I want to impact minds in a good way, make people think, and dream, and imagine.

The work on the store was extended by a few months. On the one hand, the construction on the part of the contractors on minor details like, oh, sheet rocking walls, setting up electrical boxes, and getting the plumbing working, were taking forever. Then there were all the inspections the town had to make, which the store would have to pass.

In time, we had the center of the space completely filled with furniture that had been constructed, boxes of product, and more. Then there was the flooring itself.

Originally, the floor was going to be a wood laminate. Torrance acquired a lot of pieces, since, like all other aspects of the store, we would be doing it ourselves. The concrete had to be as evened out as much as possible. As we learned, nothing in the building was even, or straight for that matter.

Well, the boxes of flooring material were not light. Also, there were dozens of them.

Initially, while the first stages of construction of the building were going on and we could not get in, Tori and her sister got a storage unit near her sisters' house, in Hudson County, almost forty minutes from the store. Eventually, while some items could be moved to the store itself, others had to move to a storage space closer to the store.

So we moved the floor. I think there were a dozen of us for that move. The flooring thus was shifted to the other storage unit. In the fullness of time, the construction reached a point where we could begin to put the floor down.

Now the flooring had to be moved to the store. This time we were seven or eight. When it came to how the laminate was packaged, no one could handle, between the bulk and weight of the packs, more than three at a time. Grab one to three packs. Move the flooring to the truck, repeat. Get to the store, lift the flooring, move to the back of the store, repeat.

One afternoon soon after that, I began the process of putting the flooring down.

I discovered two very interesting issues as I went to do that. Even though we had removed all the bumps and bits that were along the concrete floor, it was still by no stretch of the imagination, flat. As if that wasn't enough of an issue, we realized that we had two different kinds of wood laminate flooring - and of course, they assembled differently. The cursing that ensued between Tori and me and her sister would have made our grammar school teachers faint.

It was totally unacceptable. The company who sold us the flooring was called and asked to take it back. This time, however, they had to come and retrieve it. We were not moving the bloody flooring once again.

They sent one guy and a truck. That guy was not the sharpest tool in the shed. Neither was he terribly strong, nor did he have with him something useful to help move the stuff, like, say, a hand truck.

So, we moved the flooring *again*. Lift the flooring from the concrete floor at the back of the store, move it to the moron and his truck, watch him struggle to load it back up. We called ahead to let them know that, anything arriving broken was not our fault, but their driver was clueless, and likely loaded it wrong in the first place. So ended the saga of the laminate floor. Once more, when dealing with certain vendors and tech support people, I am left with only one question. Where do they find these people?

Chapter 44 – No ending, just the chapter concluding this story.

In September of 2003, Tori and her sister opened the doors to her store and spa, and soon the world would begin to discover the unique space that was *East of the Sun, West of the Moon.*

November of 2003 would be the fourth anniversary of my accident. Over the course of those four years, my life had been changed because of, and in spite of, the accident.

So who am I? What do I want from this world I was so nearly taken from, and given a second chance to live in?

It's a goal of mine to be an altruistic soul. Pretty lofty, no?

When I was first presented with the notion of telling my tale, I had to ask, well who will read it? Who the fuck am I? I am, frankly, a great big nobody.

But as my friend said, does it matter? There are plenty of regular people out there who might find my story, and my humor inspirational. Maybe people want to hear this kind of story from someone not so different from who they are. Interesting notion. I am not entirely a normal person, per se, but I am also not a celebrity, nor anyone of note. I am like any other person you pass on the street. What wisdom can I impart, and is it worth it for you to take the trek up my mountain to receive it?

I have learned a lot about myself, about the human spirit, the soul, the mind, and the body through my ordeal. I have learned that love is a powerful tool. I have learned the importance of believing in yourself, and believing in your own powers of mind and spirit. I understand why alternative therapies can work so well with standard Western medicine.

I hope that you never have to learn how precious life is by nearly losing it, or losing a valuable aspect of yourself. Believe me, it is not something I would wish on even the asshole who thought bowling me over with a car would be an interesting idea.

I have a lot of chapters which I could add to this story. This is by no means the end of my tale, this is just one very momentous volume in the story of my life. I am not writing this as a farewell, or an ode to the accident victim. I am just sharing my story. I hope you have enjoyed my tale, and take something of it with you.

OK, so I need a big finish. A really catchy ending. Something flashy, something unique!

Or maybe I'll leave it open, since this really isn't the end.

Epilogue. You can't go back again, but then, why would you want to, really?

Ten years ago, this was the first work I managed to complete for National Novel Writer's Month (NaNoWriMo). That was seven years after my accident, three years beyond where I end this tale of my life.

I have resisted sharing this story for a lot of reasons. To some degree, I am embarrassed. I did some pretty shitty things back then, and holding a mirror up to yourself, even your self from nearly two decades ago, can be a bit disturbing.

To some degree, I don't know if I want this to be what I might become known for. I love to write, in whatever form that takes, but this was a one-off. My love is fantasy and sci-fi, and my Consciousness Creation blog. Still, any work I might be able to share, and any way in which that might help someone else in some way is still a win.

Someone asked me, if I could go back in time and stop myself from getting hit by the car, would I? Truthfully…no. I am the man I am today because of what happened all those years ago, and I am stronger for it. I gained perspective and depth of experience that I am hugely grateful for. Sure, if there had been an easier, less painful means to the end, that might have been great…but as awful as the pain and recovery were, I am a better person for that part of my life.

I debated placing more than an epilogue here. I have numerous interesting tales I could add from the intervening ten years since this was finished the first time. However, I think this particular story, and the span it covers, stands alone.

A couple things of note, perhaps, to the astute reader. Everything that is portrayed here is true. It happened. The names are different, a few of the places relocated some, but otherwise all of this truly happened, to the best of my recollection, as I have written it here.

Still not giving the real names, but the following stories are true: Marnie and Leroy got married, and have a wonderful child together. My niece is pretty amazing.

Tori and her sister's store thrives, and has grown organically and exponentially to thrice its original size. Their two-room spa is now eight rooms, and the retail store is double its original size.

Both sets of parents, my mom and stepdad and my dad and stepmom, are doing well.

Sadly, Bob passed away several years ago, and I will always miss him.

Although I repeated this particular bit frequently throughout the story, I can now say that I no longer suck at relationships. I met an amazing woman, and despite having read this story prior to my current edit of it, she still agreed to date me, let me move in with her, and eventually she married me. We've been happily living together now for over five years, married for two, and our two cats are delightful monsters.

****

As of this writing it is July, 2017. Life is pretty damned amazing. No matter its ups and downs, the good and bad and ugly and orgasmic, there is always something new to experience. While I hope that you have never had to go through what I did, if you do ever find yourself in such a tough spot, know that you are not, and never will be, alone.

"The journey of a Thousand Miles begins with a single step."

- Lao Tzu

(Photo Courtesy of MBH Photography)

About the Author

MJ BLEHART was born in Golden Valley, Minnesota. He has been writing stories in the genres of high fantasy and sci-fi/space opera throughout his life, the first when he was nine years old. He currently resides in northern New Jersey.

He is a history aficionado. MJ has been a member of the Society for Creative Anachronism (SCA - a medieval re-enactment society) for over twenty years, where he studies and teaches 16th century rapier combat (fencing), enjoys archery, court heraldry and all things Elizabethan England and more.

Check out MJ Blehart online

MJ is a regular blogger – check out
The Ramblings of The Titanium Don:

titaniumdon.com

MJ's author's website:

mjblehart.com

MJ's YA Fantasy series The Source Chronicles:

sourcechronicles.com

The Steampunk world of Amasheer:

vaporrogues.com

Follow MJ on twitter **@mjblehart**
and on Facebook - **mjblehart**

www.ingramcontent.com/pod-product-compliance
Lightning Source LLC
Chambersburg PA
CBHW060922040426
42445CB00011B/747